Striving to be champion

*BABE DIDRIKSON ZAHARIAS*

Compton's Bookshelf—Great Lives

Striving to be champion

# BABE
# DIDRIKSON ZAHARIAS

by *Helen Markley Miller*

Illustrated by Richard Mlodock

F. E. Compton & Company, Publishers
Compton's Pictured Encyclopedia
Chicago • Toronto

# TABLE OF CONTENTS

Page   Chapter

7      1.  Determined to Win

19     2.  The Olympics at Last

38     3.  Making a Living at Sports

58     4.  Mastering a New Game

68     5.  Winning the Crowds

78     6.  A Memorable Game

96     7.  An Amateur Again

105    8.  A Time of Sorrow

114    9.  Setting New Records

126    10. Another First in Golf

141    11. The Beginning of Trouble

151    12. A Need for Courage

159    13. A Hard Battle Won

171    14. Back on the Circuit

183    15. "A Wonderful Life"

Chapter *1*

# Determined to Win

Babe Didrikson wriggled her wiry body through the throng of latecomers still pushing toward the gates of Northwestern University Stadium. People turned to look at her, curious because she was dressed in track suit and running shoes, but she was oblivious to their stares. Babe was late and she was in a hurry.

Breathlessly giving identification to the gatekeepers, she sprinted toward the corner of the field where she could see the contestants already gathered. A voice on the loudspeaker began giving preliminary announcements, and an excited stir ran through the crowd. She glanced up at the bleachers. All those people, she thought, so massed together up there that they looked like blobs of dark and light, had come here to see girl athletes from all over the country compete for honors in track and field events. And she was one of those girls.

Fierce determination flamed in Babe's mind. She was going to win the national championship, and she would earn a berth this fine summer day on the United States track team.

[7]

Nothing was going to keep her from going to the 1932 Olympics out in Los Angeles.

Among the contestants, she strode up to a girl who had smiled a welcome.

"Well, I reckon I made it all right," Babe panted out.

"You're pretty late. How come?"

"Taxis. We couldn't find one that'd fetch us from Chicago way out here to Evanston. And then when we did get one, I was so scared I'd be too late to change here that I put my track suit on right in that old taxi."

The girl looked shocked, and Babe had to laugh. "Oh, it was all right. My chaperone held a blanket up around me."

"The Golden Cyclones," the girl said, reading the letters across the front of Babe's sleeveless running shirt. "Where you from?"

"Texas. Dallas is where my club is, but I'm really from Beaumont. I just work in Dallas—for an insurance company. I'm Babe Didrikson."

"Oh, that one."

"What do you mean—that one?"

"I've heard of you—that's all. Where's the rest of your team?"

"I'm it. I'm the only one the insurance company sent."

"You don't mean you're going to try to compete all by yourself?"

"I'm not goin' to try. I'm goin' to do. And I'm goin' to win me a place on that Olympic team too."

The girl lost her friendliness and her eyes narrowed. "You're pretty sure of yourself, aren't you, Texas?"

"Sure I'm sure. I didn't come all this way to lose."

The other girl shrugged and walked away. Babe looked after her in astonishment and hurt. Now what had she said that was wrong? She'd only stated a fact, and this girl had turned all huffy. Sometimes other girls were mighty hard to understand. Usually before a meet they'd pretend they were no good, and afterwards, if they'd won, they'd say it was only because they'd been lucky. That wasn't honest. When she was certain she was going to win, she always said so. And she didn't go blaming loss or victory on luck either, because it wasn't luck that made an athlete win. It was skill that came if you practiced long and hard.

A little on the defensive, Babe squared her shoulders and looked around at her competitors, husky girls all of them, in teams of fifteen to twenty. She glanced down at her own scrawny legs and arms. A hundred and five pounds of weight and five feet six inches of height didn't add up to the body of a brawny athlete. She shrugged her bony shoulders and firmed her chin. Maybe she was small and skinny, but she was lithe and strong. Her body had the strength and resilience of a bull whip, the endurance of fine steel. Height and weight, she told herself, didn't make an athlete win any more than luck did: determination had a lot to do with victory. And hadn't she been set on making the Olympics ever since she'd been a youngster?

The announcer began calling out the names of the various teams and, as he did so, the girls ran out in groups onto the field. Babe almost lost her confidence when she saw that the Chicago Athletic Club had sent a team of twenty-two girls. How could she total up points all alone against a big team like that one?

"THE GOLDEN CYCLONES OF DALLAS, TEXAS," the loudspeaker blared.

"This is it," Babe muttered to herself. "That's me. Well, here goes nothin'."

Out onto the field she sprinted, waving her arms cockily at the crowd in the bleachers. A one-girl team, she kept telling herself, had as much right to compete as the larger groups did.

For a moment there was a surprised silence that gave her a queer lonely feeling. And then the crowd burst into a roar of cheers that sent little bumps of gooseflesh popping out all over her arms and legs.

"Well, I guess they kind of like me," she whispered to herself.

She was pleased, grateful to these spectators who must be cheering her not because they thought she'd win, but because she looked so thin and young, because she was willing to pit her lone self against the big teams.

"I'll have to show them what I can do," she muttered. "All those nice people."

Showing the crowd what she could do was going to be no easy matter, she soon discovered, because, in order to keep the meet running smoothly, events were being called off rapidly. In most of them only one or two girls on a team participated while the others had a chance to rest; but Babe, who had insisted on entering eight of the ten events, was kept racing breathlessly from one contest to another. First she'd answer a call from one part of the field to run the qualifying heat of the eighty-meter hurdles; then she'd scurry across the ground to take one of her trial jumps. Always she was kept running here, running there. Just getting around on time, she thought grimly, was going to keep her warmed up and exercised plenty.

She failed to qualify for the hundred-meter dash finals by only two points, but she shrugged off that loss. After all, she'd never been too good at just running. She'd always been one to go flying up into the air for the jumps and hurdles. Wait until those events came long, and she'd show that crowd of people who kept right on cheering for her.

She knew that she was good enough at the jumping to take possible first places, but there were two other contests, not her specialties, that gave her concern.

Back in Dallas her coach, Colonel McCombs, had said, "Babe, I know you haven't practiced much on discus throw and shot put, but maybe you can do well enough to pick up a point or two for the Cyclones. You won't win, of course. But do your best."

She'd just have to give that old discus and shot all she had, she decided, because it wasn't going to be enough today for her to win only the events at which she knew she was good. From now on she had to place high enough in every single contest to rack up points to make her total score a big one. Near wins added to real ones might fix it so that she could take this whole big meet. And wouldn't that be something?

Spirit high, she stepped up to take her turn at the discus throw, but she soon realized that she was competing against girls far stronger and more skilled than she. However, she surprised herself by taking fourth place to pick up one of those points she was working to gain. Now if she could do as well with the shot put. . . .

She gave the shot a tremendous heave—and herself a bigger surprise than her placing in the discus had given her.

"WINNER—BABE DIDRIKSON. THE GOLDEN CYCLONES OF DALLAS," the loudspeaker announced. "THAT LITTLE GIRL FROM TEXAS WHO'S A WHOLE TEAM, WITH A HEAVE OF 39 FEET, 6 AND A QUARTER INCHES."

Man, I actually took that old shot put event, she thought. And I didn't expect to.

"That's one first place," she muttered aloud.

And she promptly proceeded to win another first with her baseball throw.

"Two," she counted, remembering with a crooked grin the times she had played baseball with the neighborhood boys back in those days when she was still called Mildred Ella. At first they didn't want "any ole girl" playing with them, but they soon found out that she could run faster, jump higher, and throw a baseball farther than any of them could.

"Golly," they said, "Mildred can throw as good as Babe Ruth."

And Babe she became, a nickname that had stayed with her through the years, a name that she was resolved should some day flash across the headlines of the world.

Not that she hadn't put that name up in headlines already, she thought. Twice she had been named All-American basketball forward, and she had broken three records in national track competition. Even if she was only eighteen, she was listed in *Famous American Athletes of Today*. But in this meet she was getting a real chance to make that name big, and if she were chosen for the Olympics—well, the Games would offer even a better opportunity.

At lunch that noon she was too excited to eat. She was glad that her chaperone, Mrs. Henry Wood, seemed to understand that chatter wouldn't be welcome. Babe couldn't think about anything but the afternoon events.

"Can't you relax a little, Babe?" Mrs. Wood asked finally. "After all, you've done very well this morning. And you're sure to do even better this afternoon. Your best three events are coming up."

"But they're the ones that are goin' to count the most for puttin' me on the Olympic team. I just have to place high in all of them. I'm not goin' to lose out on those Olympics."

Out onto the field she ran that afternoon, more determined than ever to place high. And she exceeded even her own expectations. Again and again the loudspeaker announced the name of Babe Didrikson as winner. The crowd cheered her now, she knew, not for her courage, but for her victories. In the javelin toss, the broad jump, and the eighty-meter hurdles she was the winner. In the high jump she tied for first with Jean Shiley, an experienced athlete who was touted to win. And that afternoon Babe broke three world records—the hurdles, the javelin throw, and the high jump.

When the long day was over, she was tired, sweaty, and dirty, but she was triumphant when she ran to her chaperone.

[*13*]

"I guess I did all right," Babe said, not even trying to hide her exultation.

"All right? Babe Didrikson, you've won this whole big track meet all by yourself. Everybody's talking about you."

Babe grinned. "How many points did I make?"

"Thirty. Thirty! And the Chicago Athletic Club—twenty-two of them—came in second with only twenty-two points."

Babe laughed happily. She knew she had made an astounding record. She had placed in seven out of the eight events she had entered, won five of them outright, and tied for first place on the sixth. Now she was the national woman track champion, and her place on the Olympic team was assured.

"There are some reporters here that want to talk to you," Mrs. Wood was saying. "Will you see them?"

Babe had been interviewed after some of her basketball victories, and she didn't mind the newsmen. They crowded around her now with their notebooks and pencils, their usual questions. And then one reporter asked her a different one.

"Miss Didrikson, what gave you the ability to take this whole track meet all by yourself?"

She hesitated. He ought to know that it was a natural talent for athletics plus perfect muscular co-ordination—and training, training, training.

"Work," she told the reporter grimly. "Just plain darn hard work."

He wouldn't put that in his yarn, she knew. He'd think up something dramatic or clever, like "the lanky girl with the courageous spirit," or "the Lone Star tomboy with the gray-green eyes and hair the color of sand." Reporters had to make their stories colorful, and there wasn't much color to hard work.

That evening in happy wonder she read the sports reviews in the papers, clipping the stories to send home to the colonel and her father and mother.

"It was the most amazing series of performances," said the United Press, "ever accomplished by any individual, male or female, in track history."

She couldn't help feeling proud of herself. She was a "super athlete" and "that wonder girl from Texas." She was "The Babe," and she had arrived at the top. Or almost at the top, she reminded herself. There were still the Olympics, where she would have to compete with world-famous athletes.

To celebrate victory she danced that night with her chaperone and friends.

"Aren't you tired, Babe?" Mrs. Wood asked at midnight.

"Me? Tired? I should say not."

"Wouldn't you like to go back to the hotel and go to bed? You've had a strenuous day."

"Not me. I'm so happy I could dance under the moon all night— if there is a moon up over all these big Chicago buildings. I'm on top of the world—right up there with the moon. Or anyway with the stars."

Babe never relaxed her rigorous training, not even when she was on her way to Los Angeles with the other girls who had been chosen for the U.S. Olympic team. All the way to the coast she persisted in taking exercises, doing hurdle bends, and jogging the full length of the train through the long line of coaches.

"Why don't you rest when you have a chance?" one of the girls asked her.

"Not me. I don't need rest. I need work. You don't win Olympic gold medals by resting."

"Oh, do sit down. It makes all of us feel tired to see you jumping around the aisles like a jackrabbit."

Babe complied because she did not want to annoy the other girls. For a time she sat and watched ranches, deserts, and mountains race by the windows. She was certainly getting to see a lot of country, she thought. All the way up to Chicago from Texas, and now half across the continent to the Pacific Coast.

She remembered the time she had first heard about the Olympic Games. It was when she was fourteen, and her father had brought home newspapers that told the story of the Olympics held in Amsterdam, Holland, that summer of 1928. Even as a little girl she had wanted to be an athlete, but it was right then that she reached a final determination. She could remember narrowing her eyes, setting her lips, and thrusting her chin forward, the way she always did when she was making up her mind.

"I'm goin' to be in those Olympics next year," she announced in firm resolve.

Her father smiled fondly. "You'll have to wait awhile. They only hold them every four years."

"That's all right. I can wait. Four years'll give me lots of time to train. Man, those Olympics are goin' to be fun. I'll be right there. I'm goin' to be the best darn woman athlete in the whole world."

In California at last, Babe wasn't particularly happy during the preliminary weeks of training. Although to the newspapers she was still "the wonder athlete" who had won a national track meet single-handed, many of the older girls in the Olympic quarters had competed internationally and had traveled all over the world. With them she felt young and green. When the train had pulled into Denver to make connections for the West, she had honestly expected the town to be built a mile up in the air. Wasn't it called the "mile-high city"? And the girls had laughed at her for being such a "little know-nothing."

Girls, even athletes, Babe decided were sometimes hopelessly silly. They spent good practice time curling their hair; some of them even wore lipstick. She couldn't be bothered. She had whacked off her hair like a boy's, had it shingled close up the back, and wore it slicked over her ears to keep it out of the way when she jumped the hurdles.

The other girls flew into tizzies when they were to meet movie stars like Clark Gable and Will Rogers, Janet Gaynor and the two Normas, Shearer and Talmadge. Babe thought getting excited about meeting important people was silly too. After all, they were just nice folks. She'd met a lot of them since she'd been in California, liked them and was at home with them—more so than she was with some of the girls.

Because she felt a little lonely and unwanted among her

[17]

competitors, a little different from them, she began acting cocky, even exaggerating her Texas drawl because she knew the others ridiculed it behind her back. One day she marched up to one of the contestants and announced, "Ah'm goin' to whup you." She didn't mean to be rude or unsportsmanlike; she was just stating the truth as she saw it. She was better than that other girl and she knew she was going to beat her. But a sportswriter overheard the remark, and after that, Babe's publicity wasn't quite so wonderful for a time.

There was trouble with the Olympic coach of the girls' team, because he wanted to change her style in the hurdles.

"I can't change," she protested. "I'm used to doin' it this way. If I try a different style now, I won't do well."

"But your form's all wrong. Your front leg is supposed to go over the hurdle extended straight out, and you always crook yours for some reason."

Babe grinned. "I reckon I know the reason. I learned that way. When I first made up my mind to be in these Olympics, I started practicing on the hedges between my house and the corner grocery. Seven of them, and they were two feet across and mighty high and prickly. I crooked my front leg to get over, or I had scratches all over me—just like a fightin' tomcat."

The coach had to laugh. "Do it your own way then. Maybe you're right at that. It's pretty late in the day to change technique."

"Maybe I don't look very pretty goin' over," she told the coach, "but I'll bet I can jump those hurdles high and fast my own way—and beat all the other girls too."

Chapter **2**

# The Olympics at Last

The first day of the Tenth Olympiad came at last. Babe was impressed and thrilled by the color and drama of the opening ceremonies in the great stadium.

The flags of many nations drooped from their high forest of poles, then caught the breeze, and unfurled their bright colors against the blue California sky. In the stadium thousands of people cheered as the athletic youth of the world, men and women of all races and creeds, formed for their march before the tribunal of honor.

In the Parade of the Athletes, Babe moved proudly along, adjusting her stride to keep time with the stirring music of the massed bands. Here she was—Babe Didrikson of Beaumont, Texas, actually marching with the athletes chosen to defend the honor and glory of the United States, her four-year-long dream now a reality. She glanced ahead to where the flag of her country was borne. Farther ahead she could see the banners of thirty-eight other nations preceding their marchers, each athlete dressed in the distinctive Olympic uniform of his or her country. With satisfaction she looked down at her own trim parade jacket and skirt, proud of it because it meant that she was on the United States team. She felt noticeably small among all these husky girls and brawny young men, but she knew that she was all hard muscle and limber-jointed bone. Lifting her head high, she stood tall to listen to the official opening of the games.

A lively fanfare of trumpets announced the raising of the Olympic flag above the stadium. The five bright circles—red, green, blue, black, and yellow—linked on the field of white represented the five continents joining together here in the friendship of sport. Beneath the circles was a motto that she could not see from the distance, but she knew the words: *Citius, Altius, Fortius*, meaning Quicker, Higher, More Strongly. That was the way she was determined to run and jump and throw in her three events. She would run faster in the hurdles than she ever had before, sail higher over the bar of the high jump, and send her javelin flying with all her strength.

When the flocks of pigeons were released, she caught her breath at the beauty of white wings against blue sky. Always she had read all she could about the Olympics, and she knew that, when the Olympiad was first started in Greece centuries ago, homing pigeons had been set free to carry to city, village and countryside the news that the Games had opened and that there must be peace in all the land for their duration.

Wings still fanned the sky when the runner bearing the

Olympic torch entered the stadium, saluted the reviewers' stand, and circled the arena, torch held high above his head. Mounting the steps of the peristyle, he kindled the flame in the great fire bowl. Babe felt choked and tight in the throat as she watched and thought of how in ancient times the sacred fire that was never allowed to die was carried by some great athlete to the arena to burn there until the victors had been crowned with the laurel wreath. Nowadays, of course, the winners didn't get a laurel crown, but medals, gold or silver or bronze, that would last forever. And Babe Didrikson, she resolved, was going to carry home at least one of those gold medals.

The band struck up the Olympic hymn, and as the chorus sang the words, she whispered them over to herself;

*Happy the man chosen for fame:*
*The palm of victory on his brow shows him to the*
    *crowd's acclaim*
*He shall taste for his reward the joys divine:*
*Let the Muses crown his head*
*And let an immortal song*
*Add to the glory of Triumph and the beauty of Youth*
*The Victor's name.*

Babe smiled at her own thought as she listened to the closing words. She had youth all right, although certainly no beauty, but she was going to do her best to win "the Victor's name."

And then the speeches began. As she listened to the droning voices, the minutes dragged on into an hour, the parade jacket was too warm—and Babe's feet hurt. She fretted at the feel of stockings on her legs for the first time in her life, and the white oxfords that she was told she must wear pinched her toes unmercifully.

"Nobody's feet ought to hurt this much," she muttered to herself.

Impulsively she stooped and took off a shoe, wriggling

*Babe took off her shoes and wriggled her toes.*

the toes before she removed the other oxford. Smiling a lopsided, wide grin at the girl next to her, she winked and pointed to her stocking feet. The other girl giggled and promptly took off her own shoes, and soon all up and down the line white oxfords rested beside relieved toes.

"Looks like I started something," Babe whispered to

her neighbor. "Anyway we're all comfortable now."

"Feels a lot better. I'm tired of standing."

"So'm I. This speech-makin' is a lot of hooey anyway. Us athletes will be worn-out before we get to the contests, and it's the contests we're here for—not speeches."

Babe's interest, however, picked up when the speakers wore themselves out with words at last and the flagbearers of all nations formed a semicircle on either side of the rostrum while a young man from the United States team advanced to repeat for all the athletes the solemn Olympic oath

> "We swear that we will take part in the Olympic Games in loyal competition, respecting the regulations which govern them, and desirous of participating in them in the true spirit of sportsmanship, for the honor of our country and the glory of sport."

Babe was too far away to hear the words, but she knew them anyway. For the honor of her country and the glory of sport she meant to give all the strength and skill she possessed; for herself too, because she wanted so much to win. Always and always she wanted to win. Sighing with relief, she slipped on her shoes. It was almost over now. Some of it had been a bore, but she knew that never would she forget the pageantry and solemnity of the opening ceremonies.

The bands played the national anthem, the flagbearers returned to their contingents, and the athletes marched from the stadium. Now for the contests, Babe thought as she strode along to the music. She was eager for competition, ready to try her skill against others.

On the next afternoon one of her events, the javelin throw, was scheduled. Impatiently she waited for the warning call from the loudspeaker, but everything seemed to be running behind schedule. It was late in the afternoon, with the sun low in the west and the stadium shadowed to unpleasant coolness, before the javelin event was announced.

Eagerly Babe ran out with the other girls, glad of the chance to get warm, for even in her heavy sweat suit she had been chilled. Not knowing exactly how to proceed, she watched the German girls, supposed to be the best in this event, throw their javelins into the ground to loosen their muscles. Babe had always thrown hers into the air for a warmup, but here on this crowded field, she was afraid of hitting one of her competitors. She had to warm up somehow, she decided; maybe she'd better try the German method. Giving her javelin a mighty downward thrust, she almost drove it into the leg of the nearest German girl. Horrified, Babe apologized and stopped her exercising, although she knew she was not sufficiently warmed in the chill air. Shivering, she waited, slapping arms against her hips and stamping her feet.

Her turn came. Stepping forward, she gave a quick look at the little flag thrust into the ground to mark the last winning Olympic distance, a German flag because a German girl had set that record.

That's an easy distance, Babe thought. Inches less than my own record. I'm just going to fling my javelin right over that old flag.

Drawing back, she whipped her body forward and let

[*24*]

the javelin go, but she was so chilled from the cold and her poor warmup that somehow her hand slipped from the cord of the handle. Through her right shoulder shot a sharp pain. She gasped, knowing that she had torn a cartilage.

Fearfully she watched the spear. Usually her throws arched beautifully in the air. This one, because of its poor start, drove low. Her heart missed a beat as she watched, but the javelin sped on, still low, but going fourteen feet beyond the flag to set a new record of 143 feet, 5 inches.

Not so good, she thought, bitterly disappointed. In practices she often had made a hundred and fifty feet. Well, she had two more tries. Maybe she could beat her first throw.

The shoulder was hurting worse now, although she kept moving it and massaging the muscles. She told nobody about her injury, however, taking her other turns in spite of pain. But the shoulder caused her to lose so much power that, although she tried hard, her second and third throws did not equal her first. Heart-sick, she decided that she had lost the first place. Grimly she told herself that maybe luck did have something to do with winning or losing, for certainly bad luck had haunted her today—the chill in the air, the insufficient warmup, the slipping cord. Now those German girls were still going to be best in this event because there wasn't an American girl who could equal her own first toss, Babe knew. Listlessly she watched the Germans make their throws. But what was this? The very best that any other girl could do did not come any nearer than nine inches to Babe's first unlucky toss.

Babe had won her first Olympic gold medal!

Proud and happy, she took her place on the winners' platform that day, the flag of the United States flying above her. It didn't matter to her that her short hair was disheveled nor that her sweat suit was unzipped at the ankle to show her worn old track shoes that she had insisted on wearing. She had won a gold medal.

There was a two-day wait before the qualifying heats for the eighty-meter hurdles were to be run off. The time passed rapidly enough with daily practices and all sorts of interesting sports events to watch—the men's track contests, swimming, diving, water polo, fencing, rowing, and even football exhibitions. Babe dashed from one to another of the scheduled contests, wishing she were a man and could enter all of them. How silly it was that there were only four track events for girls! And it was even sillier that the officials would let her enter only three of the four.

The two days passed, and she was glad that her shoulder injury did not seem to interfere with her jumping. The hurdles were her specialty, and she had no intention of failing to qualify for the finals.

The qualifying race began. Over she went, disregarding the pain in her shoulder, her tight-fitting trunks and sleeveless shirt with its United States emblem moving so fast that she must have looked a blur to the cheering crowd. That day she beat not only the Olympic record, but her own world record set at the Evanston meet. She had qualified for the finals all right, she thought in satisfaction.

The next day she could scarcely wait for the final race to begin. Over-eager, she made too fast a start and jumped the gun, forcing the officials to call everybody back for a fresh start.

She wouldn't do that again, she thought, chagrined and embarrassed. If she jumped the gun a second time, the officials would disqualify her. Better to hold back until all the other girls had started. Every muscle straining to go, she made herself wait until the slowest girl was off. Then, racing fast and soaring easily over the hurdles, Babe caught up with the pack at the fifth one, her skinny legs crooking as if she were jumping those hedges back home. She heard the roar of the crowd urging her on, but she was thinking only that there were hurdles to be cleared and time to be made up. All but one of the girls were behind her now. She caught up with the leader, Evelyne Hall of Chicago, but Evelyne had hit a rapid pace and had no intention of yielding her lead. Try as Babe would, she could not pass the other American girl. Step by step, hurdle by hurdle, the two raced abreast. They passed the finish line, seemingly at the same time.

A tie, Babe thought, disheartened as she waited for the announcement of the judges. That slow start had lost her a first place.

To her delight, however, the judges announced that she had won by a slight fraction of time, beating her own world record. Another gold medal was hers.

Spectators rose to their feet and thundered in riotous applause, a good sound to her because she knew the crowd was with her now. No longer would they be laughing at her skinny frame and boyish haircut to which the newspapers had been giving so much publicity. Sportswriters would give

[ 27 ]

While the crowd roared, Babe caught up with the leader.

her better stories now, perhaps even forget her early unfortunate remark.

As she mounted the winner's platform for the second time, she was thinking that if she could only take the high jump, she would have a gold medal for every one of her events. However, there was one competitor in the high jump whom she feared—Jean Shiley, who had tied with her for first place at the tryouts. To jump higher than Jean was going to be plenty hard, Babe decided, but she meant to do it somehow.

When the day for her last contest came, she gloated as the cross bar was moved up and up until it reached five feet, five inches, nearly two inches higher than it had been when she and Jean set a new world record at Evanston. One by one all the other contestants had dropped out of the jumping until only the two American girls were left.

"Try that height," the officials said.

Jean cleared the bar. Babe cleared it.

"We'll put it up another three-quarters of an inch," an official ruled. "That'll make you two girls work to play off this tie."

Jean jumped first, giving it all she had, but she did not get across.

My turn now, Babe thought. And this is it. I have to get over.

Kicking off with all her strength, she soared into the air, using the Western roll that was new to the judges. Up, up, up, she flew, higher than she had ever jumped in practice or competition. She felt as she thought a bird must feel rising

[29]

into blue sky. Exhilarated, triumphant, she cleared the bar with inches to spare. It was hers now—that clean sweep of all her events, that certain and complete victory she had wanted to attain.

And then down, down, down into dejection she plummeted, for as she hit the ground, the cross bar came plunking after her. She could hear the crowd in the stadium groaning. What had happened? She knew her body had not touched the bar. In her drop her foot must have struck the standard a glancing blow to jolt the bar into falling. Her wonderful jump wasn't going to count. She and Jean would have to try again.

"We'll just set the bar back to five and a quarter," the official ruled. "That'll give you girls an easy time."

Over Jean sailed. Babe also made the lesser jump without difficulty. At least she was tied in first place, she thought, and she didn't too much mind sharing honors with Jean, whom she liked. But a discussion among the judges indicated something was wrong?

"You dived, Miss Didrikson," one of the judges told her. "We can't allow your jump. Under the rules your feet have to go over the bar first, and yours didn't."

Babe could not believe that this catastrophe was happening to her. She had jumped according to the rules, and the decision was unfair. She knew that one was never supposed to argue with the judges, but this was too much to take.

"I'm sure I didn't dive," she said. "I've been jumpin' the same way all afternoon, and I jumped that way at the tryouts."

"If you have, we just didn't see it," one judge said firmly. "This time we saw you dive. The ruling stands."

Babe bit her lip and tried to control the trembling of her chin, but she managed a smile, not wanting anyone to know how unhappy she felt at losing her first place tie. As she stood on one of the lower steps to receive her silver medal, she tried to conquer her disappointment.

If you lost, she told herself, you lost. And there's no use crying about it.

Just the same, she couldn't help feeling a little resentful. Second place wouldn't be so hard to take if she hadn't known that her highest jump—four inches over the bar—had been astounding and that she had not dived on her last and lesser jump. She wasn't down on that second step because she had failed to do her best, but only because of the judges' decision.

When she stepped from the platform, Grantland Rice, the famous sports columnist, who had been consistently praising her in his stories, was waiting to talk to her.

"You had a bad deal, Babe," he told her. "From up in the press box all of us could see what happened. Your feet did go over first. We're all sure."

Feeling a little better, she made herself smile at this new friend. "Oh, well, I broke another record anyway—or Jean and I did together. I guess it's fair enough for Jean to have the gold medal."

"That's the way to take it," Grantland Rice said, patting her shoulder. "How about forgetting track, now that your events are over, and playing a game of golf with me tomorrow."

"I'd like that," she responded with a smile that was not forced.

"Okay, we'll make it a foursome. You and I and a couple of other sportswriters. I'll come around for you in the morning."

When she read Grantland Rice's column that next morning, her spirits soared from the depths of defeat, for he had written:

"Not even the great Nurmi [Paavo Nurmi, the great Finnish runner] broke three world records in one Olympic. The Babe . . . is without any question the athletic phenomenon of all time, man or woman."

She was really up there now, Babe thought. Granny—that's what he'd said to call him—had not written that she was the greatest athlete in the United States. She was "the athletic phenomenon of all time." Now she had reached the goal she had set for herself four years ago. She was the "best darn woman athlete in the whole world."

Hastily she began to dress for her golf date. What to wear? A white skirt she decided, and her new white sweater with the Olympic rings on it. The Olympic committee certainly saw to it that a girl was provided with clothing. She had been issued jackets and sweaters, all with the United States Olympic emblem, skirts and shorts and shoes, even pajamas and stockings. As she laid out her outfit for the day, quite suddenly she began to worry. What if she made an awful dub of herself at golf after all the nice things Granny had said about her in his story? Of course all sports, even at first try, came pretty easily to her, but she never had played a round of golf in her life. She remembered one time when Colonel McCombs had wanted her to go with him while he practiced driving a few balls.

"That silly game," she said. "What fun is there in chasing a little old white ball over the grass?"

She went with him, however, watched him drive a few times, and then tried it herself. Taking a stance in front of a light post, she socked that ball so hard that her club hit the post behind her on the follow-through and shattered into pieces. The man in charge of the driving range came running toward them, shouting at her all the way, and she was afraid he was angry about her breaking the club, which she had borrowed from him.

"Did you see where that girl hit the ball?" he exclaimed in excitement. "Go measure it somebody."

For two hundred and fifty yards she had driven that ball straight and true down the fairway, although she'd never handled a golf club before.

Nor since, she told herself now grimly. This was the morning she was all set to make a fool of herself. Granny wouldn't call her an "athletic phenomenon" after this day.

When he came for her and she saw that the sportswriters with him were Westbrook Pegler, Braven Dyer, and Paul Gallico, she was even more concerned. Not because they were famous newspaper men, she told herself, but because she didn't want to show off her ignorance before all these fellows who knew all about the game of golf.

[*33*]

At the Brentwood Club, where they were to play, all the men wanted coffee before they teed off, and Babe saw her chance.

"I'll go borrow some clubs," she told them.

She didn't know where to go, but they told her to hunt up the pro shop. "Pro shop" didn't mean a thing to her; however she scouted around until she found a room that looked like a shop because it had a lot of golf equipment and a big table where a man was working on a broken club.

"Is this the pro shop?" she asked hesitantly.

"Sure is, miss. And I'm the pro for this club. What can I do for you?"

She told him her name and predicament and begged him to give her a few pointers.

"Babe Didrikson," he exclaimed. "The girl who broke three records in the Olympics. I'll sure be proud to help you." He grinned companionably then. "You'll pick it up in a hurry if you're so good at athletics. I'll lend you some clubs and show you a little about stance and grip. You'll do all right."

He gave her hasty instructions, and Babe was surprised to find that the golf club felt strangely good to her hands when she gripped it, felt right and familiar somehow. Maybe she'd try this sport out when she was back in Dallas.

She was glad when the men decided that, since she was new to the game, Grantland Rice would be her partner because he was the best golfer. She really liked Granny.

"Sure," he agreed. "Babe and I can take on the three of you. Make it a best ball game, and then any of us could win."

"What's a best ball game?" Babe asked.

Grantland Rice smiled at her lack of knowledge. "That means we count only the lowest score for each hole. We'll have a chance to win, even if you don't know golf."

"I don't see just how, and you all don't know what you're gettin' into," she told him. "We're lost right now. I don't know one thing about this game of golf."

"It doesn't matter in the least," he said, laughing. "We've all been writing that you're a natural athlete. Now we'll see what you can do with a new sport."

When they won the toss and he told her that she was to drive first, she didn't know any better than to put her ball right down on the ground for her first drive.

"Look here, Babe, you're supposed to make your drive from a tee," Grantland Rice told her, sounding amused.

Embarrassed, she watched him tee up her ball for her; then, stepping up, she took a good swing at it, trying to remember all the man in the shop had told her. And it was just like that other time with the colonel: the ball sailed off for two hundred and forty yards.

Westbrook Pegler let out a long whistle of admiration. "Babe, you've been holding out on us. You'll never make me believe you haven't been playing golf for a long time."

When the others had taken their turns, she was gleeful because somehow she had managed to outdrive them all on that first hole. Most of that day her drives continued to be as long or longer than her first.

At the sixteenth hole she and her partner had a two-hole lead on their opponents. The sixteenth was a short hole,

[35]

however, and Paul Gallico made the best drive, sending his ball onto the green in one shot.

Grantland Rice pulled Babe to one side and whispered to her, "See if you can get Paul to race you up to that green," he suggested, winking significantly.

She nodded, getting his idea at once: Paul wasn't in as good condition as she was, and if she could wear him out, they'd have a chance to win.

"Look at that nice big hill," she said to Gallico. "I'll race you down and up it to the green. Runnin' I mean, not playin' golf."

He took the dare, and just as his opponents had hoped, he was puffing when he reached the green, so out of breath that he had to use four putts to sink his ball into the cup.

Babe was hilarious because she and Grantland Rice had taken the match through her long drives and his steady game, although she felt a little guilty because they had won through what she called "shenanigans."

On the way back to the clubhouse he told her enthusiastically, "Babe, I've never seen a woman who could hit a golf ball the way you can. You'd make a great player—if you'd work at it."

"I think I'll do just that—work at it," she responded soberly.

'It wouldn't be easy."

"I know. But I'm used to work. Man, it'd be fun to be a golf champ."

Every new sport that she attempted was always a challenge to her, but today she had discovered one that could absorb her whole interest. Track needed strength and timing and endurance; but golf, she could see from this one day of play, would require not only those qualities, but all her intelligence and judgment as well, plus a lot of patience and even a sense of humor. Because it was a game of concentration, golf offered a new dare to her. Some day, she made up her mind, she would be as good at golf as her Olympic record had proved her to be in track.

So intrigued was she by this new sport that she managed during the last days of the Olympic Games to get in a few rounds of golf on nearby club grounds. However, she did not entirely desert the stadium because there was fun to be had there with the girls who were now her friends. And when the closing day came, she marched in formation with the other athletes, no longer feeling lonely and unwanted. She was a victor now by two gold medals and a silver, and she had made friends with interesting people.

The closing ceremonies were as moving to her as the opening ones had been. The flags of the competing nations were massed behind the speakers' dais as the Olympic banner was handed to a representative of Germany, where the next Games were to be held. Babe watched in wondering awe while the last rays of the setting sun struck the Olympic torch just as its flame died down. The band played "Aloha," and the chorus joined to sing softly the haunting words. In the stadium thousands of spectators rose to stand at attention with the athletes for a full minute after the last notes had sounded. The Games were over. The Olympic torch would not flame until another four years had passed.

[37]

# Chapter 3

# Making a Living at Sports

**B**ack in Dallas, Babe was astounded to find half the town at the station, with everybody shouting and cheering.

"What's all this for?" she asked Colonel McCombs.

"To welcome our victor home, Babe. What else?" he responded. "Dallas folks are mighty proud of you."

Soberly she looked at his kind, strong face. "Don't they know I owe a lot of my winning to you?" she asked.

Always she had been grateful to him for the part he had played in her life, grateful to the Employers Casualty Company, too, because they had given her the job that made the life of sports available to her. Colonel McCombs had discovered her playing high school basketball during a tournament in which she made twenty-six points for the Beaumont team in one game.

"How'd you like to come to Dallas and play on my team, Babe?" he asked. "The Golden Cyclones."

"Well, I'd sure like to, but—"

"I'm athletic director for all the women working for an insurance company there. We'll give you an office job with good pay. Can you type?"

"Eighty words a minute. But I'm only fifteen, and I'm not through high school yet."

"That's all right. You can come back at the end of the basketball season and finish. Let's go see your folks."

All that winter she played with the Golden Cyclones, and every winter until she finished high school; after that she became a permanent employee of the insurance company. The basketball season was always fun and excitement, and then there was a track team for the girls that she and the colonel worked up together. He was also the one who fixed it so that she could go to Evanston to try out for the Olympic team. One day she had walked into his office and told him, "Colonel, I've just got to go to the Olympic tryouts. Am I goin' to get to go to Evanston?"

His eyes had twinkled. "I've already talked the company into sending you, Babe, and they'll pay all your expenses. We're sure you'll make the team."

Babe felt now, there in the Dallas station, as if the cheering should be for the colonel and the insurance company. And yet it was for her. There was a big parade with everybody throwing confetti and long streamers of paper over her as she rode in an open car from the station to a suite of rooms engaged for her at the best hotel. The rooms were full of flowers, and people kept coming—hundreds of them—to congratulate her. Townspeople even brought her father and mother from Beaumont to share in the party.

[39]

After all the excitement of that homecoming, Babe found it difficult to settle down to work. Fiddling with a slide rule and typing letters seemed tremendously dull after winning gold medals to the acclaim of crowds. Of course she didn't have to stick with the insurance company, she told herself every day, because she kept getting other job offers and also requests to put her name on things like track shoes and shorts. Daily she was tempted to accept, but she knew that if she took money for the use of her athletic name, she would be considered a professional athlete. If she once turned pro, never again could she compete in any amateur sports contest. And yet the money that professionalism would bring. . . . She wanted money, needed it.

One night she took a long walk to think out her problems. There was no getting around the fact that she needed more money. Best just admit that and go on from there, she told herself. Particularly she needed money because there were so many things she wanted to give her father and mother to show them how grateful she was for the happy childhood they had provided her. There had never been much money in the Didrikson family, Babe thought, but there had always been a lot of love and understanding—pride, too, whenever any one of the kids accomplished anything. She thought of Dora and Esther Nancy and Ole, the three oldest ones; of Lillian and Louis, the twins, of Arthur, who was beginning to grow up. It would be such fun to buy things for all of them. And yet how could she on her salary?

Of course she'd managed a few gifts already. She grinned as she remembered the radio she had bought on credit and carried home for her father and mother. It wasn't a very big radio, and all that Christmas Eve she sat up in the day coach from Dallas holding the little radio wrapped up in a blanket to keep the case from getting scratched. When she reached home early in the morning, she slipped into Poppa and Momma's room, plugged the radio in, and wakened them to music. Just seeing the happiness in their eyes, Babe thought, was thanks enough.

And then there was that time when she was home on a visit and she saw in a store window a second-hand bedroom set, the kind her mother always had longed for. But this one was old and dark-stained, and Momma wanted an ivory-colored set. Babe smiled, remembering how she barged right into that store.

"How much for that old beat-up set in the window?" she asked.

"Oh, a hundred dollars."

"I'll give you eighty. On time. Will you take that?"

When he let her have it at her price, she asked to have it delivered to the furniture store where her father was working then. He had painted it ivory, and Momma had been so pleased she cried.

Babe sighed and slowed her pace. That was when she had been getting only seventy-five dollars a month during her first year or so of work and sending forty of it home to help her folks. Whatever she bought, even now that she was making more, had to be on credit, and sometimes it was mighty hard to make the payments. No, she wasn't making enough money. Maybe she ought to turn pro after all.

[41]

As she walked on, she passed a house with a lot of trees around it and rosebushes on the lawn. A youngster came dashing out of the door. He looked like her brother Louis, ran just the way he used to, and the house made her think of her big, sprawling home on Doucette Street in Beaumont. It wasn't big enough for the family when they moved there

*With brushes on her feet, Babe "skated" the back porch clean.*

from Port Arthur, where she had been born way back there in 1914, but her father, who had turned cabinet-maker after he quit going to sea, added rooms and a huge back porch. All the children always slept out there, boys at one end and girls at the other. She could remember the way she always scrubbed that porch, with brushes fastened to her feet like skates. And her mother never objected, as long as the porch was good and clean when the skating was over.

They'd had such a hard life, Poppa and Momma, Babe thought. Surely now they deserved whatever comforts she could buy them. Poppa had sailed the sea seventeen times, beginning with his first trip when he was only nine years old. Babe remembered how all the children gathered around when he was in a story-telling mood. There was that tale about his getting cast up on an island and eating monkeys to keep alive, and the one about the time his ship was floundering in a storm and he clung to the mast rope and kept another sailor from falling into the sea.

And Momma had worked hard all her life, too, feeding all those kids and even taking in washing when money was scarce. She was really stronger than Poppa, although he'd never admit it. Babe smiled, thinking of what her father had said when she came home from the Olympics with three medals.

"Babe gets all this athletic ability from me," he remarked proudly.

But she was quite certain that she inherited her physical co-ordination from her mother. Hadn't Momma been one of the best women skiers and skaters in her part of Norway before she and Poppa and the three oldest children emigrated to America? Then when they moved to Beaumont, times were really hard and Momma had to pitch in and help. But in spite of age and work, she still stood erect and walked like an athlete.

[43]

If only she could do more for her parents right now! She didn't want to turn pro. She didn't. And her parents wouldn't want her to, either. Best to leave things as they were. But what then could she do? Nothing except save all the money she possibly could from her salary. She could do without anything she really didn't need—like that set of golf clubs she had seen in the window of a sporting goods store. But, oh, how she wanted the feel of those golf clubs in her hands again! Golf was certainly one sport that took money, lots of money—for the clubs, for balls, for playing fees. Well, she'd just have to postpone learning to play golf.

Not long after that night a letter that seemed to settle all her financial problems came to Babe offering her a position with the Illinois Athletic Club at three hundred dollars a month. The proffered job wouldn't interfere with her amateur rating. And yet how could she leave the insurance company after its officials had been so good to her, giving her a chance to make the Olympic team, holding her job open for her until she came back? She would have to talk it over with the president. Regretfully she showed him the letter, and he surprised her by saying, "Babe, we'll just give you that much to stay here."

"Good," she answered at once, relieved and happy. "Then I'll stay. I'd lots rather. Here I'm near my folks, and everybody's my friend."

Home from work she went, thinking gleefully of all her increased salary would buy for her father and mother. Clothes first, she decided, because both of them needed clothes.

When she had saved enough, she sent her father a new

suit and some work clothes. Then one day when she was home for the week-end, she took her mother into a store.

"Momma, I'm goin' to buy you a new dress," she announced.

And when it was chosen, she said, "Now you just pick out another one."

She kept it up until she had bought eight dresses.

"Now, Momma," Babe said, eyes dancing, "that's one dress for every day in the week and two for Sunday. You've gone without for us kids long enough."

Giving to her folks was fun, and she was happy with her new salary as fall turned toward winter. One day in December she was swinging home from her work through the business district in Dallas, where she stopped to admire an automobile on display.

"Like it?" the dealer asked. "It's our new 1933 model."

"Yes. Oh, yes. It's a beauty."

"Want to buy? You can have it for just a little bit down."

"Don't you go givin' me your sales talk," Babe said. "I'll never be able to buy a car like that." And she strode on.

A few days later she opened a newspaper to see a picture of herself in an advertisement saying that she liked the dealer's new model. She thought nothing of it at the time. The dealer had seen a way to sell his cars, that was all, and he had used her name without her permission. But not long after that ad came out, she received a letter from the Amateur Athletic Union stating that she had been declared a professional for using her athletic name to make money.

Babe was bewildered, stunned. How could this happen

[45]

to her when she had been so careful. Ever since the Olympics she had been refusing all offers to advertise products, although she needed the money that professionalism would bring her. Once she even had played with the idea of asking to have that longed-for set of golf clubs given to her as a prize for an exhibition appearance she was making, but she had put the thought from her mind at once, knowing that if she ever hoped to be a big-time golfer, such a gift might automatically destroy her precious amateur standing.

Now the damage was done, and she was a professional through no fault of her own. A chance remark to an ignorant dealer—and she was no longer an amateur. Never again could she contest in the Olympics; she couldn't even play basketball with the Golden Cyclones. Their season had begun, and now she would have to sit on the sidelines to watch her teammates play. So sunk in dismay and disheartenment was she that even being chosen the Girl Athlete of the Year of 1932 by the Associated Press did not cheer her. Bitterly she decided that she might as well turn pro now in actuality, since there seemed nothing else left for her to do. At least, she thought with some satisfaction, now she could earn the money needed for her family.

The first offer she accepted was from the company making the cars that had been her downfall.

"We're sorry. Our dealer is sorry," the officials told her. "We want to do everything we can to fix up the trouble we've caused you."

She was never one to hold a grudge. "That's all right," she said. "That dealer didn't know what he was doing to me."

But it was a saddened Babe who said good-by to her kind employers and took the train for Detroit, with her sister Nancy as chaperone, to appear in the Auto Show, sign autographs, and even play her harmonica to attract crowds.

Nancy and Babe chuckled together, however, when they recalled how Babe had first learned to play the harmonica. It had been when she was a skinny youngster of seven with a Dutch bob of straight, sandy hair. One of her brothers made a radio set, and she liked to lie in bed, earphones clamped over her head, listening to her pet entertainer, Castor Oil Clarence, who played the harmonica. She was going to have one of those harmonicas herself, she decided. Since her father hadn't the money to buy one for her then, she had cut neighbors' lawns until she earned the price of the instrument.

"And you used to lie in a hammock in the back yard and play that old thing by the hour," Nancy reminisced in their hotel room in Detroit. "I can still hear you. 'Home Sweet Home' and 'Old Black Joe' and 'Swanee River.' You were pretty good at it—after you had driven us all crazy for weeks."

Babe grinned. "Sure. And I'm still pretty good. Remember how we used to have a family orchestra on our front porch nights? The boys on their drums, the girls on the piano and violin, and Momma singin.' And of course me on my harmonica."

"Sure I remember. And all the people on the block used to come out to sit on their porches and listen."

"Now I'm still drawin' crowds with my little old harmonica," Babe said, laughing.

[47]

It was true: she was drawing big crowds to the Auto Show. People seemed to like to talk to her, to hear her play and sing. In fact, she was such a success that the auto company came up with the idea of hiring an agent and getting her a contract to go on the stage on the Radio-Keith Orpheum vaudeville circuit.

"It'll be for athletic appearances," the agent informed her when he had her contract. "You'll be using your name as an athlete to make big money. Perhaps you won't want to sign when I explain what the auto company people have done for you."

He told her than that the dealer in Dallas had written to the Amateur Athletic Union to explain the mistake he had made, as had the agency that handled the advertisement. Together they had proved that she had not accepted money for that unfortunate ad.

"The AAU is reinstating you as an amateur, Babe," her agent warned her. "But if you sign for these stage appearances, you're pro for sure."

Babe thought of her family's need, and made her decision. Big money right now meant more to her than her amateur standing.

"I'll sign," she said. "I've made the step now, and I guess I might as well stick to it."

The day her show opened at the Palace Theater in Chicago, and she saw her name blazoned in huge electric letters high over the roof above even those of the popular singer, Fifi D'Orsay, Babe had worse stage fright than she had felt at the Olympics before the thousands in the stadium.

[48]

As soon as she faced her audience, however, the qualms left her.

It was a silly show, she decided, but fun. Dressed in a bright green coat and wearing high heels, she sang a song, talked a little, and played her harmonica. For the talking she had been training herself to refrain from her Texas drawl and to quit dropping her g's. After the music, right there on the stage, she had to take off the coat and the shoes, and underneath was a satin track suit. Donning rubber-soled shoes, she then went through a routine of athletic stunts.

She was an astonished girl when her "silly show" received favorable comment in the newspapers. Clark Rodenbaugh of the Chicago *Tribune* wrote:

> *Friday afternoon was the Babe's first time behind the footlights, and the girl from the Lone Star State took the hurdle as gallantly as she ever did in track. . . .*
>
> *The 'Babe' skims a hurdle, jumps a couple of times, drives imitation golf balls, and runs on a treadmill.. . . . The limited scope of the stage forbids her showing more of her extraordinary prowess, such as heaving the discus, flying the javelin or tossing a basketball. And Mildred ends her turn by playing the harmonica with no mean skill.*

"Ha," Babe said to her sister. "There's that harmonica again. I bet I'm going to get mighty sick of playing 'When Irish Eyes Are Smiling' and 'Begin the Beguine.'"

She thought it was great fun, however, to meet people

[49]

at the top in the world of sports. One night a reporter brought Jack Dempsey to her dressing room after the show. Thrilled, she told the prize fighter, "You, know, you've always been one of my big heroes."

He walked her home. It was a cold night, and they ran arm in arm to keep warm.

Toward the end of her week's engagement, she found that she was beginning to enjoy herself almost too much. If she kept on with this stage career, she was afraid that the daily excitement would get to be a habit she could not easily break. Playing to all these crowds was thrilling, yet the audiences weren't applauding the great athlete she still wanted to be, only clapping for a silly, amusing show.

"Nancy," she told her sister, "I don't think I like this stage stuff. I never get outdoors anymore, not with five shows a day. I'll get soft. I'm going to quit."

"But, Babe, look at all the money you're making. Twenty-five hundred dollars in New York next—just for seven days of work."

"I know. I'd like that money," Babe said thoughtfully. "But I think I can earn plenty with honest athletics. I don't like this way of getting it. I guess I'm an athlete, not a vaudeville performer. Besides, I'm never going to learn golf if this keeps up."

Canceling all her other bookings, she finished out her week in Chicago. She did not go back to Dallas, for there was still money to be made, only now she was going to earn it with athletics, not on the stage.

Early in 1933 she began a series of exhibition appearances in New York to demonstrate various sports. For a time then she played professional basketball with the Brooklyn Yankees, winning after one game the prize of a fat duck with a huge yellow bill and a bright green ribbon around its neck. What to do with the thing she didn't know. Taking it to her hotel with her, she filled the bathtub, and dumped the duck. All night it kept getting out of the tub to waddle, quacking, around her room. The next morning she shipped the prize duck to her parents.

When she had saved a good sum, Babe went home to Beaumont. Mother's Day was coming soon, and she wanted to buy a special gift for her mother. On a Saturday Babe shopped in one of the hardware stores and decided on an electric refrigerator and stove. All these years, she thought, Momma had been cooking for a big family on that old coal range, and storing food in an old ice box that was always running out of ice or else leaking all over the floor when nobody remembered to empty the pan underneath. Now she was going to have the best of appliances. The owner of the store was pleased with his double sale, but he wanted to wait for delivery until Monday morning.

"But I can't wait," Babe insisted. "Tomorrow's Mother's Day, and they've just got to be there."

On that Sunday morning, just to be sure that the dealer kept his promise, she went down to the store and rode home in the truck with the delivery men, leaving her sister Lillie to keep their mother out of the kitchen. The men installed stove and refrigerator, even transferring all the food cooking on the old range to the new one and moving supplies from

[51]

the old-fashioned icebox to the gleaming new appliance. Eyes dancing then, Babe called her mother, who came into the kitchen and was stunned by the glory of her new equipment.

"Don't you cry, Momma. Don't you dare," Babe begged as her mother hugged her.

"Just look at what you've done," her mother said. And then over and over in Norwegian mixed with English, "*Min* Babe. *Min* good girl."

Her mother's joy was compensation to Babe for all her time away from home doing work she didn't like; repayment enough for the sacrifice of her amateur standing. She still had eighteen hundred dollars left—a fortune, she thought. On that much money she could live for years.

"We're going to California this spring," she told her father and mother. "All three of us. You need a change, and I'm going to learn to play golf."

Still very sure of her athletic ability, she breezily announced to Los Angeles reporters, "I've a fat bankroll, enough to last me three years. And I'm going to win the amateur women's golf championship three years from now."

When the story came out in the papers, what she'd said sounded like a kid bragging, she thought, because she didn't even know how to play golf yet. She hadn't meant her statement for boasting; winning at golf was just something she intended to do. She was a little alarmed because the reporter had mentioned her professionalism, expressing a fear that it might keep her from entering amateur golf tournaments. She wasn't too concerned, however. Golf was a new field for her, and surely her professionalism wouldn't be counted against her: golf had nothing to do with the name she'd made in the Olympics at track.

With all her usual zeal she began daily practice, working by herself on the driving range for hours at a time. Progress seemed slow, however, and she began to worry because her money seemed to be dribbling away. Living expenses for three in California were not cheap.

"Why don't you get a pro to help you?" a golfing friend asked her one day. "You'd learn faster."

Babe felt green when she asked, "How could a golf pro help me?"

"Give you lessons, of course. But you'll have to pay him."

"How much?" Babe asked cannily. And when she was told, she shook her head. "I haven't got that kind of cash."

The friend, however, introduced Babe to a young golf pro, Stan Kertes, who became so intrigued when he saw that astonishing drive of hers that he offered to give her free lessons.

"No woman's going to beat you on that drive," he told her, "but you need to learn some basic things."

To her delight that very day he started by teaching her the correct right-hand grip. Until the lights were turned off at midnight, she worked on by herself, and the next morning she was was so eager to learn more that she was on the driving range before daylight, practicing until Stan came. Every day she worked at stance and grip and swing, and day after day she progressed.

But she knew that her money was running out. Instead

of the three years she had allowed herself to learn golf, she would have only this summer. Her "fat bank roll" had shrunk to just enough to take the Didriksons back to Texas.

"You won't give up on golf?" Stan Kertes asked her.

"I won't give up. This is my game, and I mean to master it. I'm just postponing. I'll be back when I've earned another stake."

Her old job with the insurance company was waiting for her in Dallas, and she went cheerfully to work. But when her father was taken ill and needed an operation, she was not only worried about him, but aghast at this new need for money. There was nothing else to do but to go back into professional athletics and forget about golf for a time.

Now began a period of barn-storming to increase her income. She played basketball with a team called Babe Didrikson's All-Americans. There were only three girls on the team; all the rest were men, and none of them were any too good, she knew. Her name, however, brought crowds and money as they toured the Middle West. When the basketball season was over, she pitched baseball for the House of David team, traveling all over the country with the bearded players. Since she knew there would be talk, she drove alone from town to town in a car they gave her and never stayed at the same hotel as the men did. Once that summer she even pitched a game for the St. Louis Cardinals. She tried tennis, hoping that it might be a sport she would enjoy, but the old shoulder injury received at the Olympics hindered her serve, although it did not seem to interfere with her golf swing. She gave bowling, pool, and billiard exhibitions, for there was not a game at which she could not excel. Golf, however, was the one sport she wanted to conquer.

The money rolled in, sometimes as much as a thousand dollars a month. One time when she was paid a big sum for an exhibition, Babe remembered the first time she had left home, on that exciting day in her life when her father took her to Dallas to join the Golden Cyclones. Traveling on a train was a wonder to her, and when Colonel McCombs met them at the station, she watched, bug-eyed, while he tipped the redcap for carrying their bags.

"Poppa," she whispered, "did you see what he gave that boy? A whole quarter! Man, I'd like to get me a job like that. I'd like to earn some quarters that easy."

Now she was earning, not quarters but dollars—thousands of dollars—and travel was only a boring interlude between one engagement and another. And yet she was far from happy.

Often she thought back to the acclaim she had won when her name first flashed into sports stories. Now her good name was gone. She was still "The Babe," but no longer a "wonder girl." When sportswriters put her into their columns now, she was "Muscle-moll Babe." They called her "lantern-jawed," remarked slyly on her bowed legs, and asserted that she was selling out her skill as an athlete to become a "cheap sideshow."

Let them say anything they want, she thought. What did they know about her reasons? She knew well why she was barn-storming: there had to be money for her family. Her father was better, but he still needed some help. Her older brothers and sisters had married, and there were nieces and nephews who would need to be sent to school; the kids had to have their chance. There had to be money for Babe Didrikson also—enough money to let her concentrate on golf. No matter what was said about her, she would keep right on being a "sideshow" until she had plenty laid by.

When her tours were over at last, back she went to the faithful insurance company. Yes, they said, she could have her job back, and if she still wanted to learn golf, they would see that she had a membership in the Dallas Country Club. They would pay for golf lessons too.

"If I ever get anywhere with golf," she told them earnestly, "it will be because of you. Every time I'm out of work, you let me come back. And now you're giving me a big chance to learn my pet game."

Not only to repay their interest in her, but to satisfy the fiery urge to play golf well that now burned within her, Babe worked at the country club every hour she could spare, practicing until dark and getting up at dawn to put in a few more hours before time for the office. Her game was improving steadily, she knew.

By November, deciding that it was now time to put her golf to the test, she entered her first competition—the Fort Worth Women's Invitation Tournament. When the day for the qualifying rounds came, she felt sure and confident.

"What do you expect to shoot today, Babe?" a reporter asked her.

She looked at him soberly. "I think I'll shoot a seventy-seven."

Her statement wasn't bravado; she had merely said what she thought she could do. And sure enough, when she had played her first eighteen holes, her score was exactly seventy-seven.

That night she read the headlines with relief and joy. The sportswriters had forgiven her the barn-storming, and she was once more the "wonder girl" making her "debut in tournament golf."

But the "wonder girl" did not have quite the experience and skill that she needed, for in the tournament match play that followed she was eliminated in an early round. The newspapers were quick to point out her faults.

"I'll get them, both—the experience and the skill," she muttered to herself, setting her chin firmly as she read the story. "I've won my name back. Now I''ll just work and work until I'm right up there at the top in golf."

Chapter *4*

# Mastering a New Game

Babe knew that she had the extraordinary muscular coordination that had always made any attempted game or sport come easily to her. She was a natural athlete, as the papers said. But she knew also that even the natural athlete can never become a great one without adding to physical aptitude certain other qualities of mind and spirit: the patience to persist against odds, the will to work endlessly, and an indomitable determination to win—not necessarily to win over others, but to master the sport itself.

She wasn't afraid of work. Every sport that Dallas offered she had tried—and labored hard to master each one. Sports might be easy for her, but partial mastery wasn't enough: she had to reach perfection, or get as near to it as she could. She played softball and billiards, handled an aquaplane skillfully, won diving events in swimming meets. In every sport she excelled, and she knew why—the undeviating effort to reach superiority.

She chuckled to herself, remembering the answer she

had given that Evanston reporter after the Olympic tryouts, the answer he hadn't put in his paper along with all those high-sounding names he had given her. She should have told him about the long and grueling hours she had spent getting ready to make the Olympic team. In the afternoons when other girls on the insurance company track team quit after their two-hour practice, she always ate a hasty dinner and then went out alone in shorts and tennis shoes to work on her timing for the jumps, or to run until dark, jogging her hard-muscled legs high to condition them for the hurdles. Learning the new Western roll that took her easily over the bar of the high jump wasn't easy either. Time and again at first she merely dived over the bar, knocking it down as her body crossed it, but she had never stopped working until her feet went over the bar before the rest of her.

This game of golf, she told herself now, was going to be even harder to master than track and field events had been. But golf promised big rewards: if she could conquer it she would develop judgment, perhaps learn to laugh at her own errors and defeats. The game offered a real challenge, just because it was so difficult to master.

She knew what she had to do. Too many times she had been forced to postpone her golf efforts in order to earn money. Now she must forget finances to labor consistently toward the aim she had set for herself—to become a champion woman golfer. The next big tournament, the Texas State Women's Championship, was set for April of that year. She would enter that meet, and in the intervening months she would work as she never had before.

[59]

And work she did. On week-end days she always managed to spend from twelve to sixteen hours on the course. This was not time enough for her, however. Rising before dawn on working days, she was at the driving range to give herself three good hours of practice before rushing to the office. Even her lunch hour she put to use. After bolting a

Babe practiced hitting golf balls into her boss' armchair.

sandwich, she spent her noon rest time practicing putts on the carpet in the office of her boss, studying her grip and stance in his full length mirror, or chipping balls into his armchair, which she always moved carefully away from the windows. Even her sympathetic boss might not be pleased with a broken pane. As soon as three-thirty came to free her from office routine, she was out on the links to take an hour's lesson from the pro and then to drive balls until dark when she went home to dinner. And every night, as long as she could keep awake after so much fresh air and exercise, she sat up in bed studying the golf rule book until she knew every rule by heart.

Sometimes she drove as many as a thousand balls a day in her effort to reach perfection in the different kinds of shots. Often her hands were bloody from blisters, but she merely taped them up and kept on working until the bandages also were bloody.

"What are you trying to do, Babe?" the pro asked her. "Kill yourself? Take it a little easy."

She shook her head. "I can't. I've been trying to master this game of golf for two years, off and on. A little thing like sore hands isn't going to stop me now. I mean to be ready for that Fort Worth tournament."

April came, and Babe signed her entry slip with a few qualms of doubt. Listed as a professional by the Amateur Athletic Union, she wasn't certain that she would be allowed to play, but the AAU had control only over track and basketball, and her entry was accepted without question.

In the qualifying round the first day she did not do as well as she had hoped—an eighty-four for the eighteen holes, and she had hoped to be in the seventies. However, she had qualified for the match play the next day. Through the match playing, with each won hole counting instead of the number of strokes, she drove her way easily. The quarterfinals were harder, although she won her round.

Her semifinal round was played on a wet and windy day. Golf was a difficult game at any time, but with the greens all soggy from the rain, shots today were going to be hard to control. She was gleeful when, at the tenth hole, she was two up on her opponent. But down her spirits plunked when she lost her lead at the fifteenth hole. The score was tied now, and in spite of all her efforts it remained that way until just before the eighteenth hole.

As Babe teed up for her last drive, she warned herself that this ball had to get up there on the green in one shot. A good long whack was what she needed. But although she drove with her usual strength, her ball went into a grove of trees, and it took two more shots to send it onto the green, still twenty feet from the cup. Her opponent also had some bad luck, and with the game still tied, the two of them took their turns at putting.

Babe held her breath as she watched her competitor's ball roll straight and true for the cup. Would it go in? No, it had stopped at the very edge of the hole. Her turn now, Babe thought, and this one putt had to be the only one. An uphill roll for the ball too, and the grass was soggy wet. Carefully she surveyed her putt from the side and then from directly behind the ball. Then, nerves steady, she made her miniature swing. And that blessed ball rolled and kept right on on rolling until it was in the cup.

She had won the semifinals!

Watching women caught their breaths and some of them cried; men cheered and shouted in relief. Babe smiled at them, knowing that they were with her because she was young and inexperienced. Calmly then, she picked up her ball and walked off the green.

That night when she read the Associated Press story of the tournament, she smiled again to read that she was "still America's wonder girl and probably the most promising woman golfer in the United States." That wasn't all the story said, however: the writer had prophesied that she would lose in the finals, since she would be playing against Peggy Chandler, who had taken the championship of Texas three times.

"Maybe," Babe muttered to herself. "But I'll be right in there driving every minute."

The next morning, although the showers had stopped, the sky was still a sodden and depressing gray. Nevertheless, Babe started the thirty-six-hole match with spirits high, and they soared still higher when a gallery of several thousand people began following her play.

She finished the first hole ahead by three, but her exultation left her when she lost the second. For a time then it was hard playing, the score teetering back and forth between the two girls. By the twelfth hole, however, Babe had hit a lucky streak and was leading by five holes. But from then on nothing she could do in that morning play seemed to be right, and the first eighteen holes of the match ended with Peggy Chandler one stroke ahead.

Babe was not too dispirited. True, she had blown up in the last holes, but the afternoon was coming with the other eighteen to play before the match would be decided. She still had a chance. She was even more determined to win when she overheard some men talking.

"How can The Babe expect to win?" one of them asked. "She lacks experience."

"Sure," the other responded. "That drive of hers is a wonder all right, but she's folded up now. She can't beat a veteran like Peggy."

Oh, can't I? Wait and see, Babe thought.

When the afternoon round started, the sun came out to dry the fairways, leaving puddles only in the hazards. She began by playing a steadier game, and although her ball seemed determined to land in spots hard to shoot from, she was finding it easier to get out of her difficulties. Unfortunately for her, Peggy was playing a good game also. Back and forth the score shifted, with the crowd shouting and cheering in wild excitement. On the thirty-fourth hole, with only two more to play, the girls were tied.

Peggy got off a good drive, but Babe stepped up to her tee and whammed her ball two hundred and fifty yards down the fairway. She was triumphant—until she saw where her ball had landed, in a ditch that cut the middle of the fairway. Trouble again, she thought, as she watched Peggy's second shot come to rest safely near the edge of the green.

That does it, Babe thought. One more shot and Peggy'll be on there. Well, all I can do is my best.

Taking a long three-iron and a wider stance, Babe whacked her ball up out of the ditch with such force that it went hurtling right past the green and landed in a roadway used by trucks. And when she went to find it, there it lay in the bottom of a deep rut, nestling cozily in water and mud.

A tough lie, for sure, Babe thought. It's going to be plenty hard to get it up out of there and on the green.

Peggy played her third shot, sending her ball onto the green close to the pin. One more easy stroke and she'd have it in the cup.

Babe knew that her winning the tournament depended now on her handling of her own more difficult shot. Carefully she studied it, trying to remember everything she had ever been told. She didn't dare make another mistake. She'd have to take her time to think this shot out.

"When you get yourself into trouble," her coaches had told her, "play percentages. If you're doing well, take a chance. Otherwise, give yourself that extra stroke and play safe."

She certainly wasn't doing well, Babe reasoned, but she had to take a chance just the same. No extra stroke for her. With only two more holes to go, she didn't dare lose this thirty-fourth one. As she took her stance, she murmured instructions to herself.

"Use sand wedge. Stand on your left foot. Call on your common sense. Think, keep your eye on the ball, and swing."

She swung, and her ball came up out of the rut as sweetly as she had willed, landed on the green, and ran smoothly toward the pin.

The crowd roared, and men and women surged toward the green, so eager to see what had happened that Babe, who was in their way, was knocked flat into muddy water. But she did not care in the least, for the cheers and excited shouts of her gallery told her that her ball must have kept right on rolling into the cup.

Two more holes to go, she told herself, and I'm one up. But the rest have to be good too.

And it was good. The thirty-fifth hole was a tie. On the thirty-sixth, a long hole, Peggy Chandler took three shots to get on the green. Babe was on in two, and her third shot put her on the edge of the cup for a sure four. Peggy failed to sink her ball on the first putt.

Babe had taken her first championship, that of Texas. It was a step toward the goal she had set for herself—to become a great woman golfer. For over two years she had been laboring toward this day; now if two more, or four, or even six, were necessary, she would give them willingly. She had golf by the tail now, she told herself triumphantly; all she needed was practice and more practice to work gradually up to the head. Next she must win the nationals. And to prepare for them she would enter every one of the women's tournaments that she could, all over the United States.

Two days later, however, she was plunged from the heights of her triumph into a black deep of frustration and disappointment. The United States Golf Association, the newspapers announced, was investigating Babe Didrikson's eligibility for amateur play. Her old record of professionalism in track was being pressed as a reason for barring her from amateur golf.

For two weeks she was kept in suspense, and then the ax fell. The USGA ruled her a professional as far as golf was concerned "for the best interests of the game."

[66]

"Whatever that means," she said to herself in hurt astonishment. How could she harm a game she so loved to play?

There was furor among her golfing friends, all of whom thought the decision unfair, and sportswriters insisted that she had been given "a dirty deal." But the ruling stood.

Babe took the almost unbearable disappointment as she had taken the first eligibility edict against her—in silence. Let others talk if they chose; she would do no pleading. If she was barred from all amateur tournaments, she could still enter the Opens, those meets that invited both professional and amateur players. But there would be no national amateur championship for her, this year or ever. Grimly she told herself that as a pro she would at least have no money worries.

"I have decided to become a 'business woman' golfer," she announced to the press. "Good golf is not a male monopoly. My own case proves it. Two years ago I took up golf for the first time. I placed myself in the hands of a competent professional and I find myself shooting consistently in the 70's. . . . I'm the happiest girl in the world today, and I'm going to work my head off playing."

Chapter **5**

# Winning the Crowds

Now that she had been officially declared a professional in golf, Babe decided to make the most of the opportunities for financial gain. As a starter, she signed a contract giving permission for the use of her name on a line of golf clubs; for publicly approving them she was to be paid a set yearly sum large enough to support her.

"That'll provide expenses to take me to a few Opens," she said happily to her pro. "I'll be a champion golfer yet, even if I'm barred from the amateur field."

In July she entered the Western Open Championship for Women in Chicago. The tournament attracted a large gallery because spectators wanted to see America's famous girl athlete play in the finals against the noted English professional, Helen Hicks. The gallery—and Babe—met disappointment, however, for both she and Helen Hicks were defeated in the semi-finals.

Babe took the loss of that tournament philosophically.

She knew that she could outdrive any other woman golfer, amateur or professional, but she was well aware of her own inadequacies in the game. She needed another year of practice to make her putts on the greens as good as her drives down the fairways. She also needed to improve her short game, those shots with the irons that would get her ball out of hazards or up on the green.

And so, when she was offered a chance to go on tour to play exhibition golf with Gene Sarazen, the best male professional player in the country, she accepted thankfully. With Gene's help she knew that she could improve her skill, for he was especially good at getting his ball out of sand traps and troublesome lies, the very practice that she needed.

When the tour began, she soon realized that she was not the fine and consistent player that Gene was. Usually he took the burden of making the score, although her long drives and her reputation as an athlete always drew large galleries. When their day of play was over, she would beg him for instruction, and together they would continue to work for hours.

Babe still was slender, although she had filled out until she was no longer the splinter-thin little girl of the Olympics. She had discarded the boyish haircut, even curling her neck-length bob. When she took time to study herself in the mirror, she could see that she was not especially pretty. But she told herself that she did have a few good points—those gray-green eyes with their direct glance, her wide, cheerful smile, the long-legged, willowy figure that looked well in the sweaters and skirts she wore for golfing.

Sportswriters still described her as "lanky" and "hatchet-jawed," still spoke of her as the "tomboy" golfer. She rather resented that word tomboy. Of course, even as a little girl, she had always liked sports, but she enjoyed the womanly activities also, and always had. Cooking was fun. And when she'd been in high school, she had been as proud of the blue silk dress she'd made in sewing class as she ever had been of her prowess at boys' games. That dress had won her a first prize at the State Fair, and she had worn it as her best during her first year with the Golden Cyclones.

"Momma," Babe asked one day when she was home for a visit, "do you remember that flare skirt I made once—when I was just a kid in grade school?"

Her mother smiled. "Yes. Anna Louise from across the street gave you her old one. And you sewed it up quick one day while I was shopping. You were afraid I'd be making you give it back."

"Sure I was. You never would let us take anything that was charity. But I wanted to have a skirt like the other girls had, and this was such pretty material—hounds-tooth wool. I worked like a fool on that skirt to get it done before you came home. How come you let me keep it?"

"You'd put so much work on it," her mother answered, smiling fondly. "I couldn't be taking it away from you. You were always a good one with the needle."

"Momma," Babe asked then, "why do they keep calling me a tomboy? I like woman things."

"It was the Olympics, Babe. And the way your hair was so short, and how good you were at jumping and throwing any kind of a ball. And you were always so skinny—just like a boy."

"Well, I'm a woman now," Babe said crossly. "Girls grow up and sort of fill out. I'm twenty-one, and I wish they'd stop calling me tomboy. That's for kids. The papers have even had me playing football and boxing and wrestling and I've never done any of those rough things."

"Don't you be minding when they call you tomboy," her mother consoled. "You're my good girl. Min Babe. You and I, we know what you are."

But Babe could not put the hated epithet from her mind. She knew that she was slightly different from other girls, and yet she couldn't be anything else but Babe Didrikson, who liked sports and was good at them. Often during that season of playing professional golf with Gene Sarazen she was lonely. Of course there was golf to fill her days, and sometimes in the evenings there were boys to dance with, one who was even serious enough to beg her to marry him. He was a nice boy, but she couldn't get much interested in him —in any of them, for that matter. Golf was too much on her mind.

One time when she was vacationing in Florida, the management of the hotel where she was staying put on a dance for the guests. She didn't go because she knew that most of the girls there would be soft and pretty debutantes, the kind who always made her feel awkward and tomboyish. Instead, she pulled on her swimming suit, ran out to the pool alone, and began diving. Before long all the debutantes and their escorts had left the dance and were watching her full gainers and back-flips from the high dive.

"I guess I broke up that dance," Babe wisecracked to a bystander.

Under the bravado of that remark, however, she was aware that she was only trying to hide her own wistful desire to be like other girls. She knew that another way she covered her inward feeling of insecurity was by exaggerating her boasts and flippancies to her golfing galleries. She had discovered that spectators enjoyed seeing her clown, delighted in listening to her quips as much as they liked Gene's skillful playing and her own powerful drives.

All right, she thought. If banter's what they want, I'll give them plenty.

And so she began putting on a good show, thankful for the vaudeville training that was now a help to her. Galleries followed her around to hear what she would say next and to watch her antics. Reporters picked up her remarks. She knew that The Babe was providing newspaper color for their yarns and a new reputation for herself. Strangely enough, neither gallery nor reporters seemed to resent her boasting. The only way she could account for that fact was that they must like her because she always remained cheerful and friendly, never resorting to the least malice or spite, always taking the barb from any sharp remark by following it with a good, wide grin. Even when she was deliberately outspoken, the crowds kept right on liking her.

Thinking about her success with spectators, she had to chuckle. Maybe it came from her effort always to let what she said or did come naturally and informally. Like that time she'd been too warm playing, and she'd called all the women in the gallery to one side and asked them to stand around her for a screen while she took off her petticoat and stuffed it in her golf bag. That was informal enough, she thought. Plenty uninhibited.

She decided that she might as well keep on playing the fool. She was having fun, and the gallery was having fun. Why quit?

And so, when she made a poor shot and Gene consoled her with a "Too bad," she quipped right back, "What's too bad?" Didn't you see me make that long drive a few minutes ago? Better than yours, wasn't it?"

"You-all come in close," she would tell her gallery at the start of a match, exaggerating her Texas drawl because she knew it amused them. "Today you're lookin' at the best little old woman golfer in America."

Or she would say, "Folks, don't you go holdin' anything I say today against me. It's just to keep you-all enjoyin' yourselves. We like havin' you follow us around. Only time Gene and I object to a gallery is when it stays home."

Once she spotted a photographer trying to take her picture. "Hey," she called out, "You've got your thumb over the lens. Maybe I'm no beauty, but I'm not that homely."

When she sank a long putt into the cup, she'd say, "Ain't that pretty?"

If she missed a short shot, she'd shudder and exclaim, "Just listen to me rattlin'. A bag of bones, that's all. I'm gettin' old and can't hit 'em any more."

One day when a gallery crowded her, she remarked

humorously to them, "Sure I'm good, and I know it. But if you-all want to see me hit this shot right up there on the green, you'll have to give the lady air."

Because it always brought a laugh, she delighted in ridiculing the men.

"Don't you fellows wish you could hit a ball that hard?" she asked the men in the gallery. "And me just a little old gal."

And to her partner for the day she would say, "Come on. What's wrong with you? You goin' to let a snip of a girl pass you up all the time?"

With her opponents she sometimes let her speech have a tinge of acid. One day a man offered to let her have the first tee-off. She gave him a scornful glance, intending to wither him.

"You better take your chance to tee-off before me," she rapped out. "It'll be the last time in this match. And you'd better whack that ball good or let a girl beat you by twenty yards."

When Babe found that the gallery loved her buffoonery, she learned to do a few tricks with golf ball and club. Placing her foot in front of her ball, she'd make it jump the foot with her putter. She would lay down her clubs like hurdles and then send the ball skipping across them. Sometimes she would set up five balls on a tee to drive them one after another, adjusting the strength of her strokes so that the last ball would be in the air before the first one hit the ground. Anything to get a good laugh from the gallery.

Although her reputation for good showmanship began

to draw larger and larger crowds, she knew that underneath the swagger she was still the lonely girl, a little unsure of herself with the girls she met away from the golf course, even a little frightened by her life in a world that exploited her because of her skill. Let them use her to draw crowds, she thought often. All her tricks and foolishness were never going to make her forget her serious aim—to improve her golf game until she was ready to become a big-time professional in the few tournaments open to non-amateur woman players. From Gene Sarazen she was learning all the time. With reasonable ease now she could get her ball out of almost any hazard, her putting game was improving, and her judgment was quicker, her touch more sure. She was earning a great deal of money too, and she liked having it.

At the end of the summer she was well ahead financially after playing eighteen or so matches, and she still had her retainer from the golf supply house, plus all the golf equipment they had given her. Now was the time, she decided, to put in a full winter of practice in California.

She had a car of her own now, and when she returned to Beaumont after her tour was over, she bought another one for her father and mother. Having it would help Poppa get well, she thought. Just watching their joy in riding around in that car was fun for her.

"Let's all go to California," she suggested to her parents. "You two, and Lillie and Arthur and me. We can have a good time together while I work on my golf. We'll just take both cars and drive out there."

In Los Angeles, Babe remembered ruefully the "fat

bank roll" that had disappeared too soon on her first trip to the coast, so this time she spent her money wisely. She rented an inexpensive apartment for her family and trusted her mother to keep down the grocery bill. None of them minded being careful, for they were accustomed to frugality, and besides, it was fun enough just to be together after long separation.

Babe took lessons from Stan Kertes again, able this time to pay his fees. All the days and sometimes far into the night, as long as lights were on at the club, she practiced drives, shots, and putts. When there were tournaments that she could enter, she played in them, not always winning, but steadily improving her game. Because she knew where she was heading, she summoned all her purpose and will to keep working endlessly.

By 1938 she felt that she was ready for competition. In January the Los Angeles Open was scheduled, a tournament in which only men played. Making out an entry blank, she took it to one of the officials.

"But, Miss Didrikson," he stammered, "women never play in our Open."

"Well, why shouldn't they? Is there any rule that says they can't?"

"No. But. . . ."

"Then why shouldn't I play?" The official looked embarrassed, and she thought she knew his reason for demurring. "You're afraid I might beat one of the good men players. Aren't you?"

"Well, no but. . . ."

Babe laughed. "I'm good, but not that good. I won't beat any of those top men pros. I just want to be in there—for practice."

She saw a calculating look come into his eyes as he weakened and accepted her entry blank, and she knew that mentally he was figuring the money to be made from the big galleries she always drew.

"I tell you what we'll do," he proposed. "We'll put you in a threesome with a minister—he's also a college professor—and with a wrestler. That combination ought to bring us a good crowd."

Babe had to smile because the plan was such an obvious publicity stunt, but she didn't mind. All she wanted was a chance to test her skill by playing in a big tournament against men.

Chapter **6**

# A Memorable Game

Babe was glad there was to be no qualifying play, although only the top scoring players in the first thirty-six holes would get to compete in the finals. She would be among those finalists, she resolved.

"Come here and meet your partners, Babe," a reporter said before the tournament. "And how's chances for some good pictures for my paper?"

She liked newsmen and photographers immensely now. The publicity they gave her was a help to her career, and besides, they were a friendly crew unless they were cold-shouldered out of stories or pictures.

"Sure," she answered casually. "If I'm going to play with them, I reckon I'd better get acquainted."

She met the minister, who was C. Pardee Erdman, also professor of religion at Occidental College in Los Angeles, and he was just another friendly and pleasant man in all the long series of partners she'd had. Then she turned to meet

"Show her some wrestling holds," a reporter called out.

the wrestler. He was big and handsome and black-haired, and his smile made her heart beat faster.

"Hello, Babe," he said.

And, "Hello, George Zaharias," she said.

Then the photographers began their work. They took pictures of Babe and George shaking hands, and she was glad that her hair was soft and shining from a shampoo, that her sweater was becoming and her tweed skirt well-fitting. It wasn't that she wanted to look well for the pictures either, she confessed to herself, honest as always.

"Show her some wrestling holds, George," one of the reporters called out. "That ought to make a good shot."

His big arms were around her then, surprisingly gentle. And somehow Babe found that she was trembling. The air seemed full of electricity, and she couldn't take her eyes from this sturdy, good-natured man who was smiling down at her as if he understood her.

When the match playing began, she couldn't keep her mind on golf, but for once it made little difference to her whether she played well or not. Big George Zaharias was behind her, and she kept looking back over her shoulder, noticing that every time she did, he was looking at her.

The gallery—and it was the greater share of the spectators—followed the threesome. She knew that they must be feeling disappointed in her playing, for they had been expecting good golf from her. Somehow she couldn't give it to them. Neither could she perform any of her usual antics to amuse the crowd.

In her first eighteen holes she shot a miserable eighty-four instead of her customary score in the seventies or sixties. George Zaharias was one up on her, and she remembered what she'd always said: that she'd never fall in love until she found a man who could beat her at golf. He had even made one drive farther than any of hers, fulfilling another prophesy she'd laughingly made: "I'll be ready to go for a man who can drive harder than I can." She chuckled to herself, knowing that neither one of them had done very well that day. There were other golfers in the first round who had made sixty-eights or less. She was out of the running for the finals now, and it didn't make the slightest difference to her. All that mattered was that she would see George the next day when they played their second eighteen holes.

"I'll see you tomorrow," he called out as he left her.

And Babe was so thrilled at that commonplace statement that she had to laugh at herself. That night she found out that the newsmen had noticed her inattention to her game. On reporter had written:

> The only person in the whole gallery who was certain of what was going on was Mrs. Edger Richards, . . . the scorekeeper. I guess religion still pays, because the professor finished with a 75, Zaharias finished with an 83, the Babe finished with 84 and Mrs. Richards finished with writer's cramp.

Babe knew that she ought to feel perturbed over that story, but she wasn't. Tomorrow was coming, and all she could think about was that she would see the big wrestler again.

After the second day of play was over, with both of them now eliminated from the finals, George Zaharias invited her to have dinner with him and his brothers in their apartment. Thrilled, she called her mother and Lillie to tell them she would not be home for dinner. Then in her car she followed George in his, but she was so excited that she managed to get lost in traffic.

"Are you trying to get away from me?" he asked, when he had turned his car around and found her.

She shook her head. How could she tell him that getting away from him was the last thing she wanted to do?

The dinner was delicious, with George broiling steaks while she was getting acquainted with his brothers Tom and Chris. Afterwards the four talked together about sports.

When she was ready to go, George told her how he had almost refused to play in the threesome. "I didn't want to play with a girl," he explained. "Not even when they told me you were really a wonderful person."

"Oh. Then we'd never have met," she said and then was embarrassed.

"Yes we would. Somehow. Somewhere."

"I—I guess we were sort of meant to meet," she stammered.

He smiled at her and she knew his thought was the same as hers. "Meet me tomorrow at the golf course?" he asked at his door. "We'll watch the lucky ones play, even if we're out of it."

She nodded, wordless, because it seemed right to be with George every day.

When the tournament play was over the next afternoon, he asked, "How about going dancing with me tonight, Babe?" And that was right with her, too.

"Sure," she answered. "I love dancing. Come for me

early and meet Momma and my sister Lillie. I wish you could have met Poppa, but he had to go back to Texas to see to things there."

Her mother liked George Zaharias, Babe could tell right away that evening, and she was glad. It never had made any difference to her before whether her family liked her men friends or not, because they were boys who didn't mean a thing to her. With George—well, her mother just had to like him.

Between dances Babe and George talked and talked. She learned that he was twenty-nine and that his parents were Greek.

"The Fighting Greek from Cripple Creek, that's what they call me," he told her, laughing hugely. "I'm not from Cripple Creek at all, but it rimes and the newspapers like it because it's catchy."

"Where were you born?" she asked, wanting to know everything about him.

"Pueblo, Colorado." He told her how he had worked on his father's farm and then in the steel mills until he had gone to live with an uncle in Oklahoma City.

"I cleaned hats and shined shoes, anything to make a living. Then after a long time I broke into the wrestling game and began to make money."

"What did you do with your money?"

"Oh, helped my folks out. They were mighty poor."

"Just like me," she said wonderingly. "Our lives have been a lot the same. Work and dreams. Loving sports and making money from them."

She forgot all about training and early hours, and it was late that night when she let herself into the apartment. Her mother, who had worried, was waiting up for her.

"Where have you been, Babe?" she asked. "You're never this late."

"Just dancing and talking—with George."

"He's a good man," was all her mother said. And Babe knew that her mother had guessed how she felt about the husky wrestler.

After that night she dated him so constantly that their friends began to call them "the perfect couple," and there were sly remarks and hints in the sports columns. Babe didn't mind, because everything said was true: she and George honestly were in love.

"Let's get married, honey," he had said.

And she had nodded. "If you want to, George, let's do."

Finding a time to get married wasn't so easy since they would need a few weeks for a honeymoon. Each of them had commitments, she for golf, he for wrestling. They kept putting off their marriage date.

Fall came, and Babe had to take her mother and Lillie back to Texas. The day she set out on that drive, Babe felt as if she never could keep on putting the miles between her and George. The desert flashed by far too rapidly, and sometimes she found herself easing pressure on the gas pedal until the car slowed. Somehow it seemed disastrous to be going farther and farther away from George. All the way to Phoenix, where they were to visit with Dora, who was married and living there, Babe kept talking about him. Her wise mother smiled as she listened.

"You want to go back to George, don't you, Babe?" she asked finally.

"Yes, I do, Momma. I guess I just can't bear to be away from him any more."

"Why don't you leave Momma and me in Phoenix?" Lillie suggested. "We can take the train from there."

"You do that, Babe," her mother seconded. "You go on back to your George. I guess he's the man for you."

Babe was so happy that she broke speed records getting back to Los Angeles, and she almost cried with disappointment when she found a note on his door saying, "Babe, I've gone to San Francisco to wrestle." Such black loneliness hit her then that she thought she couldn't stand another minute away from him. Pounding on the door, she wakened his brother Chris.

"I want to see George," she told him breathlessly. "I'm going to drive to San Francisco right now."

"But it's late at night, and a long way there. You can't do it, Babe."

"I have to."

"Then I'd better drive you."

It was dawn when they pulled into San Francisco and found the hotel where George was staying. She raced down the corridor to pound eagerly on the door of his room. And when he came out and she felt the security of those strong arms around her once more, then everything in the world was right again.

"Why did you leave that note for me in Los Angeles?"

[*85*]

she asked him. "You knew I was on my way to Texas."

He grinned. "Well, I knew one of us had to go where the other one was. I couldn't go because I had this wrestling match. So I figured maybe you'd give in. I had a hunch that you'd be coming back."

In July they announced their engagement. After that they tried to arrange their affairs so that they could be performing in the same cities or areas, but it was difficult to do. She would have a golf tournament or he a wrestling match, and often their commitments were miles apart. The convenient time for a marriage date never seemed to materialize.

In December, when both of them were in St. Louis, George reached a decision.

"Babe, it's now or never," he announced. "We'll get married this week or we'll just call it off."

Babe was a little perturbed. Marriage was a serious step that might interfere with her golf aims, but she knew that she wanted George more than she wanted golf.

"All right," she agreed at once. "This week it is."

Determining that she was going to look her best, she consulted a dress designer and had a light blue gown, feminine and lovely, made for her wedding. When she stood up before their friends with George on December 23, 1938, in the home of St. Louis wrestling promoter Tom Packs, she repeated the wedding vows soberly in a voice that did not tremble. "Until death do us part," she said—and meant it.

After the ceremony she dropped into a chair and gave a long sigh. It was over. She was Babe Zaharias now, a Babe who would never be lonely again. George was smiling down at her, and because the sympathetic understanding between them was so strong, he knew what was in her mind.

"Do you feel happy, Mrs. Zaharias?" he asked.

"Yes," she answered seriously. "I do."

She had to cry a little then, but through her tears she was smiling. "I'm crying because I'm so happy. Oh, I'm so grateful for—for everything."

She was thinking about her father and mother, her brothers and sisters, about the happy home where love had laughed at poverty, about the wonderful gift of strength that had helped her to realize her dreams of athletic prowess. She'd had so much in her life. And now she had found George. How lucky could a girl be?

They had no time for a real honeymoon then, since both of them had appearances scheduled soon, but there would be a few days before the Christmas holidays would be over.

"Let's drive up to Pueblo to see my folks," George suggested the day before Christmas. "And then we can stop and see your folks in Beaumont on the way back."

"Good," she agreed at once. "Christmas with your family. New Years with mine. It's a deal."

Out of Amarillo, Texas, heavy snow began falling. The wind howled across the plains to pile huge drifts in the road and send the flakes whirling against the headlights. Babe watched in content, hypnotized into drowsiness by the swirl of the snow. Inside the car was a warm little world, safe because George was with her, but soon the wind plastered a white film across the windshield, so thick that wipers could not remove the load. They drove on for a time, George with his head out of the window in an effort to see the road. His hair and eyebrows were covered with snow.

Babe chuckled. "I used to dream when I was a kid of riding along behind Santa Claus and his reindeer. I'm one up on that dream now. I'm married to Santa Claus."

"Maybe we'd better turn back. This is pretty bad."

"Oh, let's go on. We'll pull out of it soon. And anyway it's fun."

But the snow came down harder than ever. The drifts were higher in the road now, and often George had to rock the car to loosen it from the clinging snow. One drift proved too much for the car; it stalled and died, its transmission broken.

"What do we do now?" Babe asked, not too much concerned, for George was there to manage a rescue. She had complete trust in him.

"Nothing to do but go see if I can find some help. You stay here."

With the heater off, the car soon cooled in the icy blast of the wind. Wrapping a robe about her, Babe huddled down into the seat, wishing that George would come back. Funny how lonely and insecure she felt without him now, she thought. How had she ever managed her life alone? All those years of barging around the country. All those years of taking care of herself, getting herself out of difficulties, working for little money and big. Now there was George to take care of her. Wonderful knowledge! Wonderful feeling!

More of a Santa Claus than ever, he returned after a time to tell her that he had found a house back from the road.

[88]

"Not a sign of a light," he said, "but maybe the folks there have gone to bed. We'll get them up. Let's take a chance."

Through the heavy drifts the going was slow, but Babe felt her spirits rise with activity and struggle. It had never been fun for her to win through anything that offered no challenge. In golf she could always play better when the going was tough.

She laughed out loud. "We should have taken our golf clubs out of the car and made skis out of them."

"Did you ever ski?"

"Tried it once. I was visiting some friends near a ski hill. I did pretty well too getting down those hills too, until I got to going too fast and there was that fence looming up at the bottom."

"What did you do?"

"Jumped it, of course. And I landed in a smother of snow at the bottom all tangled up in my skis. Skiing's fun. We'll have to learn it some day."

It was a long quarter of a mile to the house, and she had reason to be glad of her strength before she saw the dark bulk through the falling snow.

"Pound on the door good and hard," she suggested. But there was no answer to all their knocking. "Do you suppose it would be all right to break in?" she asked, shivering in the wind.

"Sure. It's an emergency, isn't it. I'll find a window."

"No, wait. Let's try the door first.'

She pushed and was delighted when the door opened

under her touch. She fumbled for a light switch, found it and snapped, but there was no electricity. George lit a match, and in its flickering light they could see a large living room.

"A fireplace," he said, relieved.

"And logs. Lots of logs. We'll soon be warm at least."

He built a fire, and in its warmth they thawed and grew drowsy as they sat waiting for the owners to return. He fell asleep in his chair, and she laughed at the honeymoon she was having. Taking the robe which she had worn around her shoulders from the car, she settled down on the sofa. A few hours later they awoke.

"Those folks aren't coming back," Babe said. "If they intended to be here, the electricity would be on. I'm hungry. Let's go see if there's any food around."

They built up the fire again and then explored kitchen and icebox by means of lit matches. Finding no food convinced them that the owners of the house had gone for a long stay. Babe searched the cupboards, turning in delight to hold up three cans of pork and beans.

"Our Christmas Eve supper," she told George cheerfully. "I guess now that we can eat, we'd better plan to spend the night here. You go get a suitcase from the car, and I'll heat up the beans."

Humming to herself, she found a pan, dumped in the beans, and set them over the coals of the fireplace. Some day she'd show George that she could cook a real meal, but tonight beans were going to taste mighty good.

And then she thought: it's Christmas Eve. The night deserves more than beans eaten out of a pan.

With more matches she explored until she found china and silver, a red and white checked tablecloth, and best of all, a white candle in a holder. She dragged the kitchen table to the living room, putting it close to the fire, spread the cloth, and set the table. Then, chuckling, she found a big bowl,

*Their first Christmas dinner was—canned beans.*

turned in the steaming beans and made a centerpiece of them, flanked by the one candle.

"Merry Christmas, honey," she called when George came in out of the snow. "Our first together."

Early the next morning they were awakened by the hum of a snowplow far in the distance. Soon it came up the driveway, pushing the snow aside in two great waves.

"There's a car coming behind the plow," Babe exclaimed. "Our hosts, do you suppose? Whatever will they think of us for breaking in?"

But the R. L. Bowens, who owned the house, were happy that their uninvited guests had found shelter.

"We saw your car stranded in the drifts back there," Mr. Bowen said, "and we were hoping that you'd found our house and made yourselves comfortable."

"We didn't leave any food here because we planned to be gone for some time," Mrs. Bowen said. "Whatever did you find to eat?"

"Pork and beans," Babe responded, laughing. "The best Christmas dinner I ever had."

She liked the Bowens at once, and before she left knew that she and George had made two new friends.

That Christmas adventure was not the only honeymoon, Babe had, however. The next spring George came in one day to announce, "Pack your duds, Babe. We're going places."

"Where? Florida?"

"Never you mind. Just put in clothes for warm or cool weather, and let's get going."

By this time she was accustomed to her big husband's impulses to travel. Sometimes he would wake her early in the morning to say, "Get up, honey. We're going to California," or to wherever his fancy led him. And she would always say, "Okay, honey. Let's go."

This time she thought she knew where they were going, because once when they'd talked about having a delayed honeymoon, he had asked her where she'd like to go, and she'd said she thought it would be nice to take a "slow boat" to Australia. George always tried to get her everything she wanted. And sure enough, that's where the boat they took was headed, after a three weeks stop in Honolulu. George had bought first class tickets on a luxury liner, and Babe was soon bored with formality.

"Let's move down to third class," she suggested. "It's dead up here. Much too stiff. And I'm tired of dressing for dinner every night."

Down in third class she began having a good time with a troupe of entertainers on their way to keep an Australian engagement. There were tightrope walkers, acrobats, tumblers, singers. "Real athletes, like us," Babe said. Every night she and George would join the troupe for singing, and she hauled out her harmonica to accompany their mandolins and guitars. This was more like the honeymoon she had wanted than the formality of the upper deck she thought.

Since there had been little time for golf after her marriage, she had put on weight. Now she was hoping to get in some good practice in Australia. When she mentioned it to George, he chuckled. He had already made arrangements to schedule golf exhibitions for her and wrestling exhibitions for him.

All over Australia Babe played golf in the large cities, driving from one to another in a small English car that had been given to her and George. She laughed at him when he had trouble getting his huge frame into and out of the seat, and both of them chuckled delightedly over a cartoon that appeared in one of the papers. The artist had pictured the car mired down in mud with George stuck in the seat while Babe, "that magnificent specimen of athletic womanhood," as the papers called her, pushed the car from the rear.

Australians had not believed the stories of her golf prowess until they saw her play, but after her first exhibition the newspapers unbent enough to praise her long drive and her skill with the trap shots. Sportswriters called her "that really delightful girl" and said that her golf was "impressive." Galleries began following her around the fairways as they had in America. On good courses and poor she played in sunshine or in rain, and when she came within one stroke of the record set by their best man professional, Australians were ready to concede her extraordinary skill at the game.

Everywhere she was in demand. One day she and George drove to keep an engagement in the back country.

"I wish we hadn't come," she told him. "Look at that course. The grass is all dried up, and there are big cracks all over the greens."

When she went into the club house, she was still more disturbed, for it was dilapidated and dirty, cobwebs festooning walls and furniture. She felt better, however, when she saw horses and buggies and wagons outside and realized that these people must have driven miles to see her play.

"We'd closed this course down," a man told her. "But when we had a chance to get you here, we cut the grass and did our best to fix it up for you."

Touched and grateful, she gave them the best playing

she could. And when she was invited into the club house, she was astonished to see what the women had accomplished while she played. They had cleaned it, decorated it with ribbons, and set tables with white cloths, tea, cakes and cookies.

"All that work just for me," Babe said on the way back to the city. "I guess they really wanted to see me play." Silent for a moment, she went on thoughtfully. "George, if it means so much to folks to watch my golf game, then I've got to get back into it, work harder than ever. I've been much too lazy."

A few days later she was unhappy over one story in the papers. The reporter had said, "If Miss Didrikson tightens up on her short game, she may get a place among the best men professionals in golf."

"May?" Babe snorted. "They have the word wrong. I will. And I'm going to start right now."

Chapter 7

# An Amateur Again

In Australia everywhere were evidences of World War II, which was fast approaching. Soldiers marched in the streets, airplanes buzzed overhead, shortages in food and clothing made purchases difficult. All the talk was of war and that man Hitler.

"Let's go home," Babe proposed. "America's bound to get into this before it's over, and we ought to be in our own country to do what we can."

Back in Los Angeles they bought a two-family house, moving into the downstairs unit. For a time Babe was satisfied and happy as she furnished their apartment, thoughtfully buying beds and armchairs large enough to be comfortable for George. After her early years of skimping, it was a satisfaction to be able to buy only the best in furniture, rugs, and appliances, knowing that George was making good money with his wrestling. She bought the sewing machine she always had wanted and made her own drapes and curtains because she enjoyed doing work for her home. She made all her golf shirts, shorts, and skirts, creating the patterns herself so that the clothing would allow her the proper freedom for her swing and drive. She worked hard on her lawn, planting the roses she had always loved. Momma was fond of roses too. Babe thought of how cross Momma used to get when the neighborhood boys and girls played baseball in the big back yard on Doucette Street! The ball was always being knocked into the roses, and then Momma would come running out to scold. One day they persuaded her to play a game with them, and she smacked the ball right into the middle of her cherished bushes. After that she never complained when one of the gang had an accident.

Babe also began improving her appearance at this time. She chose dresses that were more feminine, gave herself a permanent by following the directions on the box, and even used lipstick.

Changing her looks, keeping a house, fussing with her roses, and cooking her mother's recipe of Norwegian meat balls for George weren't enough for Babe, however. She kept up with her golf and kept herself fit. She began to think about competition again.

"George," she said one night, "here I am with a good golf game all cooked up. And what am I doing with it? Playing exhibition matches now and then. Never getting to compete in any tournaments."

"You play. Don't you?"

"Sure I play. But that isn't enough for me. It's no fun unless you can put yourself up against others. No challenge

[97]

to it. And there just aren't many tournaments open to professional women golfers."

"Two," he reminded her. "There's the Western Women's Open. And the Texas one."

"I know. And I'll enter them, of course. But two a year isn't enough to keep me sharp. I'm getting rusty. Staying at the top in any sport takes more practice than it does to get up there. I need competition to keep me on my toes."

"Ever thought about trying to get back your amateur rating?"

"Could I, George? Oh, do you suppose I could?"

"I don't know. But I'll find out for you. Anything you want, Babe, I'm always going to try to get for you."

He began to make inquiries about the possibility of regaining her amateur status, consulting with Pardee Erdman, the minister who had played golf with them on the first day they'd met. He was now an officer of the United States Golf Association.

"You can do it, Babe," George reported, "but it won't be easy. You've been pro almost five years, and that means you'll have to get in your application for re-instatement before those five years are up. That'll be in May. After that time you're pro for good."

"That's easy," Babe said, all excited and happy. "Is that all I have to do?"

"Not by a long shot. Then you have to go through three years without doing anything that could be considered professional, like taking money for anything connected with sports. It's a sort of probationary period. Can you do that?"

She thought it over. Giving up all the money she made from her contracts with sporting goods companies and from exhibition matches wouldn't be easy, but after all George was earning enough so that they really didn't need her addition to the family income. And she could still play all the open tournaments provided she didn't accept any prize money.

"Of course I can do it," she answered. "And I will do it."

By January of 1940 she had her application in, accompanied by letters of endorsement from prominent amateur golfers. She wrote a letter of her own to the secretary of the USGA to tell him that she didn't want to be professional any more now that money was no longer a necessity, and that she wanted to play golf only for the fun of the game. When a letter accepting her application came, she was delighted. At once she dropped all her money-making contracts, canceled all dates for professional appearances, and began her three-year period of probation.

Now, with more incentive than ever to practice her golf, she began spending many hours on the links. In the year of 1940 she entered the Western Women's Open in Milwaukee, refusing the prize money and putting her name down on the entry blank as Babe Zaharias.

"I'm Babe Zaharias now," she told George, "and proud of it. I'll never enter any competition again as Babe Didrikson."

She won that tournament, the first big one she had played since 1935, shooting a seventy-two to set a new record for the course in Milwaukee. In October she also won the

Texas Women's Open at Fort Worth, competing against many of the best amateurs and professionals.

"Looks like I'm still hitting the top," she told George as gleefully as a little girl.

The few tournaments she could enter, however, were not enough activity for her, accustomed as she was to living vigorously. To fill in the time between golf competitions she decided to take up tennis, now that the old injury from the Olympics was entirely healed. She began taking lessons from Eleanor Tennant, who had taught Alice Marble, one of the best women tennis players. With her customary enthusiasm for a new sport, Babe played sixteen or seventeen sets a day, rubbing holes in her socks and wearing out the soles of her tennis shoes.

Soon she was beating her teacher and playing often with women tennis stars or with some of the best at the game among the movie actors—Peter Lorre, Paul Lukas, or John Garfield. In the fall of 1941 she felt that she was ready for tennis competition and entered her name for the Pacific Northwest Championships. Again, however, she had to accept disappointment. Once she had been a professional in any sport, she was told, she was always a pro for tennis. Babe hung up her racket and quit the game. Without competition, the challenge of playing was gone for her.

"Golf's my real love anyway," she told George. "And besides, now I'll have more time to help you."

Delighted because he had decided to retire from the wrestling ring to please her, she threw all her vitality into assisting him in his new projects. When he opened a custom tailor shop in Beverly Hills, for a time she ran an establishment for women's sports clothing next door. When he became a wrestling promoter, she helped by selling tickets. When he decided to investigate bowling alleys with the idea of buying one, she took up bowling seriously. George did not make the investment, but she kept on playing. Here was a game that had no rules barring professionals, and in it she could compete as much as she chose.

"Your right hand will get too strong," George warned her, "and first thing you know, you'll be hooking all your golf shots. Bowling could wreck your golf game."

"No it won't," she insisted, and kept right on playing until she had set some new records in bowling.

When America entered the war after Pearl Harbor, Babe found a new outlet for her vigor—benefit golf exhibitions with the proceeds going to support war charities. Both she and George wanted to do all they could to help along the war effort. Many times he tried to enlist, but was turned down by every branch of the military service because of his wrestling injuries.

"That settles it," he told Babe after his last attempt. "And I thought I could do a lot of good—teaching those boys to defend themselves when they'd lost their guns. Wrestling holds, you know."

"We'll do all we can anyway," she consoled him. "I'll play all the exhibitions they ask me to."

One of her war relief matches was with Babe Ruth, the great baseball player, whom she had met earlier in her career. She had told him then how she had come to be nicknamed Babe, and he had been her friend at once. He had advised her, since she was making money at that time, to put some of it into an annuity against the time when she would be too old for athletic activities.

"Do you remember," she asked him before they played, "telling me to buy an annuity?"

He nodded. "Good advice too."

"Maybe, but it didn't work out for me. I got me an annuity, and then I kept increasing it until I couldn't make the payments. I lost that old annuity. I guess I'm not a very good business woman—or wasn't then. I was just a green kid making lots of money. Only trouble was that I had too many places to put it."

"Know better now, Babe?"

"I sure do. George and I are doing mighty well. We own our own home, a farm in Pueblo, and property in Denver. We're investing what we don't need. I guess all us athletes have to grow old some time, and it's a good thing to be prepared."

Sometimes Babe played with movie stars like Mickey Rooney and Johnny Weismuller, the Tarzan who was such a favorite with the youngsters. Most of all she enjoyed playing with Bing Crosby and Bob Hope. She loved their clowning, remembering all her old tricks to keep the gallery amused. The two movie actors were certainly much funnier than she ever had been, Babe decided.

Once when she teed off to send the ball for two hundred and eighty yards down the fairway, Bob Hope flung himself face down on the ground, beating it with his fists,

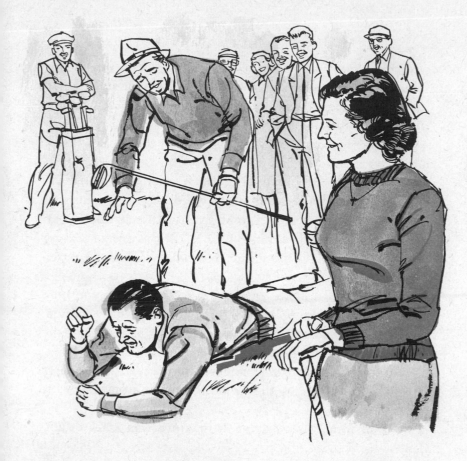

Hope flung himself down and beat the ground with his fists.

while Bing put on an exaggerated act of consoling. Another time when Bob had failed twice to make an easy eight-foot putt, he remarked to the gallery as he took his third stroke, "This is still the same man putting." And when the scores were announced at the end of the match, Bob began singing "Jeannie with the Light Brown Hair" as loudly as he could so that the gallery could not hear that his score was so much worse than Babe's.

"I hit the ball like a woman," he told the gallery. "Babe hits it like a man."

No one in the crowd cared much whether the golf was good or not if they could listen to the drolleries of Bing and Bob. Babe, for once in her golfing years, was not the big attraction, but she didn't mind, because all three were playing for a cause in which she believed. Besides, she, too, enjoyed the fun.

She was glad, however, when three years from the time she had sent in her application for re-instatement as an amateur, she received a letter saying that she had successfully complied with all regulations.

"Now that I'm an amateur again," she told George happily, "I'm going to start concentrating on getting ready for the Nationals."

"You mean you're going to give up war relief exhibitions?"

"Not for a minute," she answered. "Any time they ask me to do anything that might help bring this war to an end, I'll be right there."

Chapter **8**

# A Time of Sorrow

Eagerly Babe began her training. As a professional she had been barred from the Nationals; now she wanted fiercely to become United States champion in golf as she had been in track. In addition to daily work on driving range and putting green, she played with other good golfers as often as she could. Once she had several rounds with Joe Louis, then the heavyweight boxing champion of the world.

She also entered as many tournaments as she could, although not many big ones were being held during the war. Gas for civilian car travel was rationed, and both train and plane reservations were difficult to get without military priority. However, there were a few women's tournaments scheduled in California, and Babe won most of them.

During 1944 she was winner and medalist at the Western Women's Open, and the next year she felt that she had to be on hand to defend her title, although the tournament was to be held in Indianapolis, halfway across the continent. The time was inconvenient for her also. When her father had died two years before, she had brought her mother to Los Angeles in order to have her near. She had not been well, and Babe hated to leave. They were in the confused turmoil of a move to Denver also, for George had decided to change his wrestling promotions from California to Colorado. He insisted on her going to Indianapolis in spite of the difficulties.

She had just won one of the preliminary matches when she was told that she had a telephone call from Denver.

It's George, she thought happily. He wants to know how I came out, or maybe he just wants to say hello. She smiled, thinking how they couldn't bear to be separated long, even now after seven years of marriage. He always ran up terrific telephone bills calling her when she was away.

"Babe?" he asked. "You all right?"

"Sure. I just won a match. And tomorrow—"

"Honey, I'm afraid I have bad news for you," he interrupted. "Your mother is ill. A heart attack. It's—pretty bad."

Babe could not say a word for a moment, thinking of the mother she loved so much.

"Are you there? Are you all right?" George asked again, his voice sharp with his concern for her.

"I—I guess so. I just couldn't talk."

"I know how you feel honey. But you had to know."

"I'm coming back, George. Right away. I'll get a plane somehow."

"No, Babe, no. Your mother wants you to finish the tournament. She wants you to win."

[106]

But Babe had lost all desire for golf. With her mother ill, she had to get back. A frantic call to her sister Nancy, who was with her mother, brought the same message, "No, don't come, Babe. Momma wants you to stay and keep on playing."

"Is she—going to pull through?" Babe asked fearfully.

"We're afraid she won't."

"Then I'm coming back. What's a golf game compared to Momma?"

All that night Babe struggled in leaden desperation to get a plane or even a train reservation, but there wasn't a seat to be had out of Indianapolis. Worn from her sleepless night, distraught with anxiety, she thought at first that she would drop out of the tournament.

No, she told herself then, grim with determination, you're going to play today because Momma wants you to. If I can call Nancy tonight and tell her I've won, it will make Momma happy.

Babe told no one of her trouble. After all, it was her own. And she played in the quarterfinals that day.

"I won for you, Momma," she whispered to herself as she came from the golf course.

There was another phone call waiting for her, and Babe knew what the message was before Nancy told her: their mother had died during the night. Babe felt lost and forlorn, like a little girl deserted in the dark. She tried to find ease from her grief by action, calling as many influential people as she knew in Indianapolis to beg them to find accomodations for her to the West. She called George and set him working from the other end. She had to see her mother once more, even if the loving smile that had always held such warm welcome would no longer greet her. But war priorities came first, and neither Babe nor anybody else could get her a seat on a plane.

And so, not knowing what else to do, she played in the semifinals, tears blocking her vision so that often she had to wipe her eyes before making a shot.

Memories of her happy childhood kept coming back, those days when even the word *Momma* meant love and strength. There'd never been any inhibitions about showing affection in the Didrikson family. Babe remembered how, when she was a very little girl, she loved to crawl into bed with Momma and hug her. And Momma would say, "*Min* Babe. *Min* best girl." Always she had given of her time and energy to make good things for the children to eat. On Christmas there were cookies and loaves of Norwegian *Jule Kaka*, those good Christmas cakes. And on Hallowe'en she always made a great big pan of cookies as "trick-or treat" goodies for all the children in the neighborhood.

Babe never knew how she managed to get through that day of golf unless it was because she kept telling herself that she was doing it for her mother, who had wanted her to win. Babe knew she wasn't playing her usual game. She'd lose a hole when she began thinking about her mother, and then she'd make herself win one—for Momma. On the twelfth hole the score was tied. After that, Babe pushed grief into the back of her mind, called on all her powers, and concentrated enough on her shots to win the last four holes and win her semifinal round.

Victory was no solace, however. That night she persisted in her battle to get a reservation, but had no luck. She
simply couldn't play in those finals, she told herself. Then she
began thinking about the time when her father was out of
work and had to go to sea again for several trips while her

*Winning was no consolation to Babe in her deep sorrow.*

mother was left at home to keep the family going. Those were
the days when her mother had taken in washings and put all
the children to helping her on the scrub board and with the
ironings. She hadn't quit because she was in deep trouble. She
had just worked harder and more cheerfully than ever.

All right then, Babe told herself, you're not going to

quit either. If you can't get a plane by tomorrow, you're just going to finish this tournament and play it as well as you can. And you're going to win for Momma.

The next day determination carried her grimly, doggedly through to the very last hole. She managed to play so well that she not only won the match, but set a new course record of seventy-two during the morning round.

Early the next morning, almost as if it had been arranged that she stay long enough to win the tournament as her mother had wanted her to do, Babe's plane reservation came through.

"We don't know how far you can get," the man at the airport desk told her. "You may be put off somewhere along the way if your seat is needed for military personnel."

At Kansas City the inevitable wartime emergency occurred, and she had to yield her place to someone with a high priority. She stayed at the airport, hoping that somehow she could pick up a seat on another plane. Weary from golf and sleepless nights, she dozed at times, waking often with a start to think of her mother.

There was iron in Momma, Babe thought proudly, and some of that strength she had given to her children. Momma always made them take responsibility, always saw to it that their jobs were finished. Babe could still remember some of those tasks she'd had as a child: the twenty-eight big windows on the back porch that had to be washed and shined every Saturday, the ironing for three boys of tough khaki shirts and trousers, the shoes that must be cleaned every night before she could go to bed, the woodwork that had to be sparkling clean even in the corners. Momma had always taught them all that when a job had to be done, it must be well done—and no whining.

Babe remembered how, when she was a little older, twelve or so, she had wanted to earn some real money to help out. She packed figs in a factory at thirty cents an hour until her hands began to get sore. Then she did piece work at a factory, sewing up gunnysacks at a penny a bag. She always kept a nickel for herself and took the rest home to her mother who put it carefully away in the big blue sugar bowl. But Momma never would spend any of that money on herself, Babe thought lovingly. Whenever there was anything Babe wanted, Momma would pull the money out of the sugar bowl and say, "You go buy what you want, Babe. It's your money. You earned it."

When memories of her mother would get too much for Babe, she would pester the ticket agent to find out if a seat were available.

"Not yet, Mrs. Zaharias," he answered too many times. "But we're doing our best for you."

But at last there was a plane, and this time she managed to make it as far as Albuquerque, New Mexico, before she was again told that she must get off and wait. Growing desperate, she tried to charter a plane, but there was no gasolene for civilian trips. She called George and set him working on all the contacts he had. But it was of no use; she had to wait. Finally she was given a seat on a plane going as far as Phoenix, Arizona, but there she had another long wait with too much time to think those long thoughts that brought tears and yet somehow made her feel better about her mother's death.

There'd never been any monkey business about Momma, Babe told herself with a little smile. Sometimes it was easy to get around Poppa. If he happened to have a little spare change, he'd give it to her or one of the other kids for candy or a movie. And if she needed a pair of shoes, she always tried to work it so that Poppa bought them for her, because he'd buy good ones. But not Momma. She'd buy cheaper shoes and say they'd do just as well, the way children grew out of them so fast. She kept a tight hold on the money because she was practical and knew that there were many uses for it in such a big family.

What a lot of grief and trouble all of them had made for their mother, Babe thought, regretting her share in the mischief. There was that time when she had gone to school with a brand new dress on, and coming home she'd stopped to play baseball with some boys. Somehow she put a big three-cornered tear in her dress. When she came home late, Momma was in the kitchen hobbling around because she'd had an accident getting off a street car and had sprained her ankle. Poor Momma. With the pain and all, it was just too much for her when she saw that new dress all torn and dirty. A whipping was coming, Babe knew, and she started to run. Then she saw Momma's ankle.

"Don't run, Momma," she said. "I'll wait for you."

Babe had to smile there on the hard seat of the airport waiting room when she remembered how her mother forgot all about being cross and laughed instead.

"Aren't you going to whip me?" Babe asked.

[*112*]

"How can I when you're feeling so sorry for me—trying to save my ankle?" Momma had said.

Babe felt a little better after that memory. Her mother certainly had not had an easy life, and sometimes all those youngsters with their mischief must have been hard to take. And all the brothers and sisters, as soon as they began earning money, had done all they could to help out. Momma's last years had been easier.

At last the waiting was over and there was a plane that would take Babe to Los Angeles. She arrived just in time for the funeral, which the family had been holding over for her. The day when she saw her mother's face for the last time was her own birthday, but Momma couldn't help to make it the happy one she would have wished for her daughter. Babe wept when she was taken to the chapel where her mother was and the family left her alone for a few minutes. She looked down at the worn face that seemed so peaceful now.

"I won for you, Momma," Babe whispered softly. "And I didn't quit. I'm never going to quit when things get hard. You taught me that, and I thank you."

# Chapter 9

# Setting New Records

Babe won her second Texas Women's Open that fall; and at the end of the year another honor, one that she had not received since the Olympics, came to her. She was named Woman Athlete of the Year by the Associated Press. The citation read:

> Although Mrs. Zaharias first won fame as a track star and later competed in most sports as an amateur and professional, she now concentrates on golf. It was in that field that she was outstanding during the '45 campaign. . . .
>
> Mrs. Zaharias became the first woman to capture three Western Open titles.

In 1946, after losing one match, Babe scored three wins before it was time to begin training for the National Woman's Amateur Championships.

"I've been wanting to win the Nationals for thirteen

years," she told George. "Now I'll have my chance. And I'm not going to muff it."

Winning didn't seem nearly so difficult as she had thought it would be, although she was opposed by skilled competitors. When she made only a third place in the qualifying rounds, she was a little concerned; but after that lapse she never slipped, marching through all her matches and taking the finals by a wide margin. She was a national champion now.

During the rest of that year she added three more wins to her score, and was again cited the Woman Athlete of the Year.

Babe felt that she was ready now for a rest and a little home life. She and George had bought a house in Denver, the first real home they had ever owned, for they had shared the Los Angeles duplex with others.

"I love my house," she announced, "and I'm going to stay right here for a long time and just cook and sew and plant roses."

"Babe, you can't stop now," George argued. "Look at all the wins you have on your record. If you keep on, you can build that string of victories up into a list no woman's ever had before. Why don't you go down to Florida this winter and enter all the women's tournaments there?"

"Will you go too?" she asked.

When he was with her, she always felt more like playing. Although he could not equal her in golf, he knew the game thoroughly, and she depended on him for coaching and advice. Besides, she thought they had been separated too much.

He promised to go with her, but when the time came, there were business matters he could not leave. She drove away alone. For about a hundred and fifty miles she kept thinking about George all the time. She and George were one, even in golf. He acted as her manager, publicity agent, trainer, and coach. She knew that people liked to see him follow her around a course. She smiled thinking how he always blew smoke from his cigar to show her the wind direction, how he always came rushing up to hug her when she won. She wasn't going to go to Florida without him, she decided. Turning her car around, she headed back toward Denver.

"How come you're here, honey?" he asked.

She gave him a straight glance from the gray eyes. "I couldn't go on. I kept getting more and more lonesome all the time. It was just like that other time when I started to drive away from you in Los Angeles before we were married. I had to come back."

She knew he was pleased, but he argued her into leaving for Florida a little later. When she had won her eighth tournament in a row, counting those she had made the year before, she called George.

"I'm coming home," she announced. "I've broken a record with eight straight wins. That's enough for now."

But he wouldn't let her leave the South, promising that he would join her in another week or so. "You just keep playing the circuit," he urged. "You've hit a winning streak. Nobody's going to stop you now."

On through the South she moved, playing tournaments in Florida and North Carolina—and winning all of them.

[*116*]

Nine victories, ten, eleven, twelve, thirteen—she added to her record. She was the wonder of the sportswriters now; she was color; she was news. And all she wanted was George.

He managed to come for her fourteenth match at Pinehurst, North Carolina. Babe was playing in the finals against Louise Suggs, who was noted for her skill and her knowledge of the short course there. Winning this tournament wasn't going to be easy, Babe knew. She played a careful game, managing to be one up before the last hole.

But on that last hole, nothing seemed to go right. She teed off, and her ball landed in an impossible place—in front of a tree. Standing back, she studied the lie of the ball. If she tried to drive it toward the green, she would hit the tree with her club on the backswing. Remembering the skill she had gained at playing billiards and pool, she decided to try driving the ball toward the tree, in hopes that it would bounce back onto the green. The shot went wrong, the ball bounced far to the right, and stopped, not on the green. Disturbed and angry, she reached down to move away some straws in front of her ball, her fingers touched it, and it rolled. She had lost another stroke as penalty for moving her ball. At the end of that hole she and Louise Suggs were tied, and Babe stood to end her long string of victories. However, there were two extra holes granted to play off a tie; she would forge ahead on those. And she did, taking her fourteenth consecutive victory.

"Now I'm going home," she told George. "And nothing you say will stop me."

One whole lovely month she spent at home before going to Washington, D. C., to score her fifteenth victory, topping off the year by being again voted Woman Athlete of the Year.

And then one day George exploded a bombshell under her. "Honey," he said, "I think you ought to try for the British Women's Amateur cup now that the war is over."

"Oh, no. I couldn't," she protested. "No American woman has ever won that tournament." And then she thought about her determination so many years ago to become "the best darn woman athlete in the world." At the Olympics she had proved herself in track, but all her golf tournaments had been won only against American competition. If she could win that British cup. . . . Hastily she added, "Let's see, it's in Scotland this year, isn't it?"

"That's right," he told her, grinning because he had known she would not be able to resist an attempt to win the cup. "At Gullane. A seaside course. That'll give you a different kind of course to win on. Cold and rain and fog. That's Scotland."

All that winter she worked hard in preparation, practicing constantly on the southern links to fit herself for what she knew was going to be the hardest battle in her career. Every time a rainy or foggy day came, she hurried to the golf course, in order to be ready for play on such days in Scotland. Sometimes she wondered how she dared attempt the British tournament, but whenever she was ready to back out, some big golfer would encourage her. Bobby Jones helped her with her stroke in Georgia and told her about the time he had taken the men's amateur cup in England after a long winning streak such as she had just enjoyed. Tommy Armour, another of the great names of golf, insisted that she go.

"You go, Mildred," he urged. "It'll be the experience of your life."

She smiled because he would never call her Babe. "All right," she promised. "I'll go. But it won't be for experience. I'll go with the idea of winning. Wouldn't it be something if I could prove I'm the best woman golfer on either side of the Atlantic?"

Babe landed in Southhampton, England, on a hot and sticky day in June, 1947. From then on until she reached Scotland everything became a blur of discomfort and frustration for her. Why on earth had she worn her heavy suit and carried her fur coat? This day was a scorcher. Nobody met her to help, not even a reporter. There was no seat on the train, and she had to stand all the way to London, trying to find places to stow cameras, knitting bag, and all her luggage. Perspiring in the heat, she tried to find a taxi to transfer her to the train for Edinburgh.

"Lady," an attendant told her, "you'll have to wait your turn. Please get in queue."

The man explained to her that she must wait at the end of a long line of people trying to find a taxi. In London there still were wartime shortages, and transportation seemed to be one of them. Finally, with the minutes ticking too rapidly by, she found a taxi to take her to her station, but before she could get in to buy her ticket, the gates were slammed shut.

What now, she thought. Worried for fear she might miss her train, she asked a guard, "What's up? Why are they closing the gates?"

"It's the King and Queen. Can't you see the red carpet?

[*119*]

Nobody is allowed in the station while they are there."

In a fog of weariness and irritation, she watched the King and Queen of England walk sedately down the red carpet between the flowers that lined it.

Well, Babe thought, at least I saw the King and Queen. Now I'm going to get my ticket.

But when she started to hurry down the carpet toward the station, she was stopped by a shocked guard.

"Lady," he warned, "you must not walk on the carpet. That is for the King and Queen only."

"But I have to get my train for Edinburgh. Royalty or not, I'm going to get into that station."

The guard was patient and courteous, but he made her wait until the carpet had been rolled up and carried away. She barely made her train, and when she was on at last, again there was no empty seat.

"But I paid for a first class ticket," she protested to the conductor. "Don't I get a seat?"

He shrugged and indicated the crowded car full of civilians and officers of the British Army. "You can see. There are no seats. You should have come earlier."

As she stood in the aisle with cinders blowing in the open windows all over her, the smut blended with the perspiration that was now streaming down her face. Her hair was losing its curl and hanging bedraggled on her collar. Winning the British cup wasn't worth all this vexation. At last the first call for tea came.

I'll get in there fast, she thought. And I'll sit in a blessed chair through two or three orders of tea.

Again, however, she ran up against crowded post-war conditions. "You may sit for only one serving," the waiter told her. "Others are waiting."

When she descended from that uncomfortable train near midnight, she was weary almost to fainting from the long standing, but her sense of humor had come to her rescue. In England she wasn't "The Babe," who had won fifteen straight golf tournaments. England didn't even know who Babe Zaharias was.

Scotland knew, however, she found out when she saw a car waiting for her at the station to take her to Gullane.

"How far is it?" she asked the driver.

"Forty minutes or so, Mrs. Zaharias," he told her apologetically.

She laughed. "Don't be sorry. I'm not. I'm just thankful to sit anywhere for a while," she said as she took off her shoes and settled into soft cushions to steal the nap she'd been wanting all day.

Scotland was different, she decided, Gullane was wonderful, and the little inn where she was to stay could not have been more perfect.

"I've been wanting to meet you, Mrs. Zaharias," the combination night clerk and bellboy told her when she arrived. "I've always read anything I could find about you."

The comfortable room with its soft bed looked like a haven of refuge to her when he took her up the stairs.

"We want to do everything we can to make you comfortable," he told her. "The manager has even bought special food for you—American food."

[*121*]

Babe was touched. "But isn't everything rationed here yet?"

"Yes, of course. Purchasing was a bit difficult, but we wanted you to have what you would in America."

The next morning she told the waiter at breakfast that she would like ham and eggs, not in the least expecting to get them. But he nodded happily.

"You shall have them. We have some chickens penned behind the inn—just for you. And there are both bacon and ham. The manager found an American boat and bought for you. We're all your fans here, Mrs. Zaharias."

Babe almost cried at finding such consideration here in a country where she was a stranger.

After breakfast she walked to the golf course for a practice round. Everything she saw on the way interested her, because all was new and different. The little stone houses with the fences around their gardens looked homey and charming, she thought, and the people riding bicycles or walking seemed pleasant. In her friendly American way she said "Hello" to everyone she met and to the women who put their heads out of the windows as she walked by. Everyone seemed to know who she was, for they answered, "Good morning to you, Mrs. Zaharias." Much too formal, she thought. She would ask the reporters to put a notice in the papers requesting everybody to call her Babe.

"Stop in for tea on your way back from golfing," women called out from their windows.

"Thanks. I don't know but what I will," Babe answered the first two or three.

After that she had to smile and say she'd already been asked for tea. These Gullane people certainly were giving her a splendid welcome, she thought.

The golf course, however, was surely unlike any on which she ever had played. The roughs were thick hedges from which it would be almost impossible to whack a ball if she were unlucky enough to land one in that jumbled mess. Right then she made up her mind to avoid those hedges, which the Scottish players called "the winds." All over the course crews of Polish soldiers who had escaped to England during the war were working to bury the big cement pillars that had been set close together to prevent German tanks from making a landing on the coast. Instead of mowers to keep the grass in shape, the Scottish people used sheep, and Babe had to laugh to see how well trained the beasts were. Every time she set up a tee to drive a ball, the sheep would calmly step off the fairway into the long grass or into a bunker.

While she practiced each day, she kept noticing that along two of the fairways, which bordered streets, the occupants of the houses watched her play. In a breezy and friendly way, she waved to them. They were folks, just like the people back in Texas or Colorado, and obviously they wished her well.

She liked Scotland, and was grateful not only for the interest shown in her, but also for the many courtesies and for all the consideration she received. When she voiced regret that there were no practice fairways set aside where she could work on the same kind of shot over and over, the club secretary thoughtfully fenced off a place for her to use, turning the sheep in to eat down the grass. And she was not only thankful, but amused when he sent a man dressed in an inappropriate white coat to precede her and clean off the greens where sheep had grazed. When the long daylight of Scotland kept her from sleeping, the manager of the hotel ordered blackout curtains hung over her windows. One of the women across the street from the golf course even sent her children over to invite Babe to dinner, and she accepted happily. It was fun getting acquainted with these kind, hospitable Scottish people.

Before long she had even more reason to be thankful for their courtesy. The weather turned cold, and she had no warm golf clothing to wear. When she had packed, she had decided that she would take only light summer skirts, shorts, culottes, and two sweaters. She had thought that when she reached Scotland, she would buy what she might need for cold weather. Wasn't the country famous for its woolens? Unfortunately, she had not figured on the post-war conditions; clothing was still rationed and she had no coupons. In one of her interviews with reporters she mentioned her predicament. When the story came out in the papers, many of those bicyclers she had noticed pedaled to the inn bringing packages of warm clothing; the mail was flooded with more. Picking out a warm siren suit, the kind British war workers had worn during the bombings, and a pair of old blue corduroy slacks, she wrote to thank the donors, asking reporters to publish her gratitude to all the others.

"Please tell them all to come to the hotel and take back

what I don't need," she said. "There must be many people who could use such clothing. And please tell the Scottish people how wonderful I think they all are."

One day she had an accident rather detrimental to her playing. In trying to get a ball out of the grass in the rough, she injured her thumb. When she examined it that night, she called a doctor.

"You've chipped a bone, Mrs. Zaharias," he told her. "You ought not to play, but if you insist, then I must bandage this thumb."

"Oh, no," she protested. "I couldn't play all bandaged up." She laughed then. "Besides, all these nice people here would think I was getting ready to alibi if I lose the tournament. Fix it up some other way."

The doctor put on an elastic bandage, and every morning, busy as he was, he came to apply a drug to kill the pain. With a glove over her sore thumb, she kept right on practicing.

The opening day of the tournament, June 9, was drawing close now. Babe was surprised at the way the playing was to be managed. There were to be no qualifying matches to weed out inferior players. Instead, the names of the ninety-nine woman contestants would be put in a hat the first day, and she would play the one whose name she drew. Every day the names of the defeated golfers would be dropped, and the winners would draw again. By the finals there would be only two contestants left to fight it out for the cup. Babe was determined to be one of those two.

Chapter **10**

# Another First in Golf

A golf tournament in the British Isles was nothing like a similar contest in America, Babe decided.

The gallery was there all right—several thousand people—but all so quiet that she was bothered. Didn't they like golf? Or was it that they resented her because she was an American trying to steal the title? She was accustomed to a gallery boisterous with enthusiasm, pushing and shoving to get near the play, shouting and applauding vigorously. Here nobody clapped for her, and the most she could get out of the spectators was an occasional quiet, "Good shot," when she drove a long one or, "Fine playing," if she managed to get her ball out of a tough lie.

"What's wrong with the gallery?" she asked the woman who was acting as marshal. "I wish they'd enjoy themselves a little."

The marshall seemed shocked. "Oh, but they're being quiet out of courtesy. It would never do to interfere with a player by making a lot of noise. Order is the rule here."

Babe decided that she couldn't endure all that quiet, and she resolved that she was going to loosen up that crowd somehow in the afternoon match.

"Come on, folks," she said to them as she teed off, "have a little fun. I don't mind noise. Just make a lot of it and I'll show you some better playing."

She even clowned a bit, but still the crowd was silent. By the sixteenth hole she had taken the match by winning more holes than were still to be played. Here was her chance, she thought. In America, when a match was over before a full round was finished, the contestants always played off the remaining holes, which were then called bye holes. Since score would not be counted any more, she intended to have some fun.

"Let's play off the bye holes," she suggested to her opponent

"Oh, but we never do that here," the woman responded.

She asked Helen Holm, the British amateur woman champion. Doubtful at first, Mrs. Holm, who had played in America and knew the custom there, finally said, "Go ahead. Play them."

Then Babe really began clowning. She put a kitchen match on the ground behind her ball, and when she hit the ball, the match went off with a loud sound that brought scattered laughs from the staid gallery. Babe's ball soared for three hundred yards to land in a trap directly in front of the green. She then balanced one ball on top of another in the trap, swung, and the top ball bounced into her pocket, while the bottom one arched straight and true toward the cup on the green. The gallery was laughing and cheering, now. This was more like it, Babe thought, and she climaxed the performance by turning her back to the cup and hitting the ball between her legs directly to the pin.

She had that gallery with her now, Babe thought, as she signed autographs. Awkwardly she wrote her name, not wishing to remove the glove concealing her sore finger.

The newspapers that night told the story with humor; they also claimed that the British had never seen anything like the game and the show that Babe had given them. "OUR GIRLS SHAKEN BY GOLF BABE," one headline ran. And the accompanying report said:

> Mrs. Zaharias took practically all the spectators and crashed her way over the hills and dales of this testing, undulating course. She tore holes in the rough with tremendous recovery shots, and simply bettered her opponents in both her matches with the most tremendous exhibition of long driving ever seen in women's golf.

Babe had told the reporters frankly that this tournament was the only major golf title left for her to capture. This was the top, and she wanted more than anything to be the first American woman ever to win it. She meant to win too. Why else had she come so far?

The newsmen repeated her words and when their stories came out, one woman, a retired golfer, resented those remarks and decided to do everything she could to keep Babe from winning the cup. Babe, all unsuspecting, accepted an invitation for tea at the clubhouse, because she wanted to be friends with everybody. Over the teacups the woman began her needling.

"Mrs. Zaharias," she said, her voice sticky sweet, "there seems to be a jinx on all you American women who come

*"I came over here to win; no jinx will stop me!" Babe said.*

over here trying to take the cup away from British women. Isn't it a pity? None of your women players have ever won, you know."

Babe smiled. "Well, maybe it isn't a jinx at all. Probably it's because all those others just weren't on their game the days they played."

"Oh no," the woman persisted. "It's a jinx, I'm sure. And how can you expect to win when all those fine players couldn't?"

Babe pushed back her teacup and rose to her feet. What was this woman trying to do to her?

"I came over here to win," she told the woman flatly. "And no silly jinx is going to stop me."

And nobody seemed able to stop her. On toward the semifinals she marched, winning all her matches, often making men's par, even scoring two under men's par a few times, she outdrove her opponents by from fifty to a hundred yards, and entertained her gallery with spontaneous drolleries and adroit tricks.

Her long drive was the talk of all who watched her, and her gallery increased each day. Among her standbys she had noticed two old Scotsmen in kilts who followed her every move, shaking their heads in wonder when she drove.

"Who are those two old men?" she asked at the club house.

"Pros from northern Scotland," she was told. "All golf pros wear kilts there."

She liked the two old fellows so much that she considered playing in kilts as a compliment to her faithful fans, but when she bought an outfit she found it too bulky to give her the necessary freedom. However, she always smiled at "her boys," as she began to call them, giving them a special wave.

Newspaper publicity by this time had reached the stage of exaggeration, but she was used to that. Reporters were applying such adjectives as "spectacular," "astounding," "magnificent," and "phenomenal" to her playing.

One humorous incident reported in the newspapers concerned Babe's objection to Scottish caddies. They were all men of eighty or so, old golfers who knew a lot about the game and didn't hesitate to tell her what to do. At first she had tried to ignore any hints that her caddy gave her, but one day he had insisted that she use a three-iron when she wanted a wedge to get up on a green. Stubbornly he took a three-iron out of her golf bag and handed it to her.

"Please," she begged, "leave my clubs in the bag and let me pick up my own. I want a wedge."

"But the wind's blowing against you. You'll be needing this three-iron, or you'll never be getting the ball where you want it."

"I intend to use the wedge," she told him shortly.

That night the papers reported that she had asked the club manager if she couldn't please have a younger caddy.

"Yes, Mrs. Zaharias," the manager was alleged to have said. "We'll get you a boy."

And the newsman's tale had it that a caddy had been brought who was "only seventy years old."

Babe laughed, knowing that she had been using the same caddy throughout all the matches and had never entertained any intention of changing—in spite of the annoyance of his constant advice.

On the day of the quarterfinals the newspapers were saying that one of the final matches was sure to be played between her and Jean Donald, a Scottish girl who lived in Gullane. Babe had become good friends with this girl and had often been invited into her home. It was going to be fun to play Jean, Babe thought, not in the least disturbed when people kept telling her that Jean was a fine golfer, so much at home on her own course that she was sure to win. The harder the match, Babe knew, the more surely she would rise to the challenge.

The forecasters were right about one thing: Babe and Jean were matched in the semifinals. Not even Babe had any objections against a too quiet gallery that afternoon. Spectators were overenthusiastic in their eagerness to see the match between Scotland's favorite and the American prodigy. Five or six thousand people had gathered to watch the play, and it took a hundred guards to keep them in order.

To her own surprise, Babe had no difficulty winning. Jean seemed to be off her game, hitting her drives almost as far as Babe did, but not doing well on the short game and putting. Babe took the match with a big score of seven and five, and by the thirteenth hole it was over. She did her own inferior version of the Highland Fling, repeating it later with Jean for photographers.

George called that night, as he had been doing every evening since she had arrived at Gullane.

"Well, I'm in the finals," she told him triumphantly.

"Sure you are. I knew you would be."

She felt better for hearing his voice and knowing that he believed in her, but she was a little frightened just the same. Tomorrow's match was going to be the most important in her golf career.

"I'm scared," she told George.

"Don't be, honey. You'll win. Who's this Jacqueline Gordon you're going to be playing anyway? Never heard of her."

"She's a dark horse. She isn't supposed to be one of the best British players. Just the same, she's been beating everybody all week."

"Well, she won't beat you," George encouraged before he hung up. "Quit worrying. You can win over any dark horse."

Babe wasn't so sure. Jacqueline Gordon had been playing hot all week, and perhaps her luck would last. Babe began to think then about the jinx that was supposed to sit on the shoulders of all women golfers from America who came to Scotland to try for the cup. The woman who had been so intent on needling Babe had accosted her occasionally at the hotel.

"Remember the jinx," the woman would always say, with that honey-sweet smile of hers. "You won't be able to beat it, Mrs. Zaharias."

Babe went to bed early and tried to sleep, but the thought of the jinx kept her awake. At last she got out of bed, opened the curtains, and sat by the window looking out. Here she was, a grown woman, and she had the butterflies in her stomach worse than she'd had them as a skinny girl before the big national track meet that had sent her to the Olympics. She smiled, remembering how her chaperone had been so worried that she had called a doctor.

"Just feel my tummy," Babe told him when he came.

[133]

"It's jumping up and down just like a grasshopper."

"There's not a thing wrong with you," he told her. "You're nervous about tomorrow, and its affecting your diaphragm nerves, making them jump. Go to sleep and forget it."

Babe felt a little better there by her window, remembering that she always had butterflies the night before any big tournament, and when she suffered from them she always did better the next day. Just the same, these were worse than usual. Hoping that it would settle her nerves, she called the desk and asked to have a cup of hot tea sent up to her. When the clerk brought it, she told him about the woman and her jinx.

"Mrs. Zaharias, that's an unpleasant woman," he said. "The management has been trying to get her to quit talking to you. Don't you heed her. Everybody here likes you, and we all want to see you win tomorrow."

Comforted by kind words and hot tea, she went to sleep at last. And when the morning came, she had forgotten all about the jinx. Running to her window, she drew back the curtains on one of the most perfect days she had seen in Scotland. It was so pleasantly warm that she decided to wear a light skirt and sweater and her white golf shoes and visor. Feeling happy and confident, she went down to breakfast.

"Only ham and fried potatoes this morning," the waiter told her, apologizing for the lack of eggs. "Those hens aren't laying too well."

"There's plenty of ham here to carry me through a tough morning," she told him gaily. "You know, I'm going to win today. My hands feel skinny, the way they always do when I'm going to play good golf."

Her white shoes hurt her feet, and she went to her room to change into an older pair, smiling as she remembered those white oxfords that had pinched her feet at the Olympics until she had taken them off during the speeches. A girl had to be comfortable, especially to play a good game of golf. Longingly she looked at a pair of brown shoes that she'd had made especially for this sea coast course. They were the most comfortable ones she owned, but they were worn from being wet so much and then being dried too fast in front of the heater. Sighing regretfully, she chose another pair that never had fitted too well.

Her spirits were still high as she set out for the golf course, and they rose higher when she saw an immense crowd waiting for her, including her two sweet old Scotsmen in kilts. She smiled at them, thinking that they had come to seem like lucky mascots to her. Nothing could go wrong today.

On a pole over the tee-off the British flag flew, and she felt so good that she saluted it to the cheers of the crowd. But where was the American flag? Then she saw it over her shoulder, over the roof of the club house. Acting on impulse, as she so often did, she knelt on the ground and salaamed three times to the flag of her country. And Britons and Scots cheered for her again. With such a lovely start to the morning, how could she be anything but lucky?

But the day that had begun as warm and pleasant

[135]

changed as suddenly as Scottish weather had been doing since she came. A cold wind blew, and she became chilly, almost too uncomfortable to play well. The wind knifed through her thin sweater and swirled her skirt. If only she'd had sense enough to put those old blue slacks into her golf bag! Or better still the siren suit that always kept off the wind so well.

The cold soon kept her from playing her usual game, in spite of the challenge presented by the fact that Jacqueline Gordon was still on her winning streak. She was two ahead of Babe at the twelfth hole.

This will never do, Babe scolded herself. Forget the cold and play.

She made up the two points by the eighteenth hole to bring the score to a tie.

"Go put on your lucky slacks," one of her old Scotsmen called to her as she started to the club house for lunch. "Go get your slacks, get your lucky slacks," fifty other Scottish voices took up the refrain.

She intended to put on those slacks, and the siren suit also, because she needed warm clothing against the bitter wind. As she changed in her room, she remembered a time when she had been superstitious.

It had been back in the days when she was playing basketball with the Golden Cyclones in Dallas. One night she made a hundred points for her team at a tournament, and she was so tired afterwards that she couldn't wait to get to bed. In the elevator of her hotel she unlaced her basketball shoes, kicked them off inside her door, pulled her socks off and tossed them into a corner, and dashed for the shower. Every night all through the rest of the tournament she had gone through exactly the same routine.

Now she knew better than to be superstitious about clothing. Comfort was what she wanted, and comfort she wasn't going to have during the afternoon match—not even with the blue slacks to keep her warm—unless she could get those well-fitting brown shoes fixed before the play began.

She hunted up the shoe shop, which had a lady shoemaker, but on the door was a sign, "Closed for the afternoon. Have gone to see Babe play."

Disappointed, wearing the uncomfortable shoes, the blue courduroy slacks, baggy at the knees and sadly in need of a press, and the warm jacket of the unbecoming siren suit, Babe set out for the club house.

"Did you get your shoes mended?" somebody asked her.

"The shop was closed," she answered. "Gone to see me play. The joke's on me."

But the kind Scotch people passed the word along, and in a few minutes the shoemaker came hurrying up to take the shoes, rushed off to her shop, repaired them, and brought them back before the match began.

"Oh, I do thank you," Babe told the woman. "I'm so grateful for these good old shoes. Everybody here is so good to me."

Whether it was the shoes or the warm clothing, Babe didn't know, but she began playing her usual game, breaking the tie on the very first hole. She kept on winning holes, and although Jacqueline Gordon played a steady and consistent game, Babe soon knew that the match was hers. The British girl managed to tie a few holes and take one, but she could not equal Babe's brilliant playing.

Babe began to feel so happy that she wanted to clown a little. Looking around, she saw her two mascots eagerly following in the gallery. She had just hit a long drive from her tee to the green, but her next was going to demand a wedge shot if she put her ball in the cup. As she walked along behind her two old Scotsmen, she heard one say to the other, "I've seen all the Americans play—Walter Hagen and Bobby Jones and Gene Sarazen. And not one of them could hit a ball like this lassie."

On impulse she slipped up between them and put her arms around their shoulders. "Want to see me whack my little old ball right into the cup with my wedge?" she asked.

"That would be grrrand indeed," one of them said, his Scottish burr thick on his tongue. The other one nodded, speechless.

Selecting a wedge from her bag, she took a good swing and knocked the ball. Although she didn't quite make good her boast, the ball skittered right on the edge of the cup, where a light touch would knock it in. She smiled and waved to her Scotsmen, amused to see that they were standing perfectly still, mouths dropping open in wonder.

Those darling old fellows, she thought. They've helped me take this tournament.

On the fourteenth hole the match was over. Babe was

five up with only four more holes to play. She had won the British amateur cup for women.

Unable to control her joy, she did another Highland Fling, with the photographers crowding around to take her picture. For a long fifteen minutes the crowd stood to cheer her, not a person in the gallery leaving the course. Then there were hordes of reporters, more photographers, and people crowding around to ask for her autograph. This time, since the tournament was over and nobody could accuse her of preparing an alibi, she took off her glove to sign. Those nearest her saw her injured thumb.

"She's been playing all this time with a hurt finger," somebody said in wonder. "That's why she always wore a glove to play."

Babe grinned and cocked the thumb at the crowd, and they cheered again. By the time the photographers asked her to go to the front of the club house so that she could pose for pictures there, she was feeling so triumphant that she leapt the brown brick wall surrounding the golf course as if it were a hurdle. Everybody applauded again. When she received the big cup, the first American girl ever to win it, she stood up and sang a Scotch song that she had taken the trouble to learn hoping to please these people who had been so wonderfully kind to her. They did like it; she could tell by the cheering.

After the ceremonies of presentation were over and she was on her way back to London, she had to laugh because this trip was entirely different from her unpleasant journey to Gullane. At Edinburgh a crowd had gathered to sing "Auld

Lang Syne" to her, and on the train she was given a compart-
ment loaded with flowers all to herself. In London special ac-
commodations had been made to take her to Southampton,
with even a purser from her ship on hand to take care of her
luggage.

No more queues for me, Babe thought. I guess the English really like me now.

She was happy to be carrying the cup home to America,
but she knew that she was even more pleased because she
had won to her the people of the British Isles. Of course her
playing had been the reason for a lot of the acclaim, but all
the kindness had not been for golf alone. They had really
liked her for what she was, and she was glad that she had
been her own spontaneous self. She'd been just Babe Zaharias, who clowned once in a while, played golf with all her ability, and wanted to be friends with everyone.

# Chapter 11

# The Beginning of Trouble

All the way across the Atlantic, Babe was in a happy glow of triumph, full of the warm, rich pride of achievement, scarcely able to wait to tell George of her adventures. As the *Queen Elizabeth* approached New York, she paced the deck impatiently. Soon she saw a boat full of men coming out to meet the ship.

More reporters, she thought, and photographers, for as it came closer she could see one man with a newsreel camera. And there at the rail in front, standing high as if he would pull the boat forward with his own eagerness, stood another man, a huge one. George! He had come all the way from Denver to meet her.

Happily she waved to him and then, putting two fingers to her mouth, she whistled shrilly, the way she used to do when she was a youngster wanting to get the attention of one of her friends. He saw her and waved his joy. First man out of the boat, he began to climb the ladder, and just as he did, the deck gave a slight lurch.

*As he began to climb the ladder, the ship gave a lurch.*

"Hey, George," she called down to him in glee, "you're tipping the ship with those three hundred pounds of yours."

Before they could be alone together, there had to be two hours of interviews with news and camera men.

"I wish we could get a shot of you in Scotch kilts," one photographer said.

Babe grinned. "Always ready to oblige. You just wait a minute."

In one of her bags she had brought home two complete kilt outfits. In a few minutes she appeared dressed as a Scotch lassie, and she had even persuaded George to don the kilts she had brought for him.

To Denver she went with George, eager for home and a rest. But the city also wanted to welcome the Babe who had won the British cup. Through the streets she rode in the parade in her honor, eyes misty, a catch in her breath because all these people seemed so glad to see her. In the parade were floats to represent every phase of her long athletic career from basketball through hurdling, javelin throwing, and baseball to golf. Her own special float, filled with the roses she loved, came last. There were speeches then, and the mayor gave her a key to the city, a key so huge that not even George could carry it. So thrilled was she over her triumphal homecoming that she put her arms around the mayor and kissed him to the cheers of fifty thousand enthusiastic spectators.

Not long after coming home she won her seventeenth consecutive victory, this one at the Broadmoor Club in Colorado Springs.

"That's enough for a while," she told George. "Now I'm just going to settle down and enjoy being home."

She was not given much chance to rest, however, for her telephone kept ringing and agents of various business concerns kept calling on her to beg her to give up her amateur rating and accept promising money-making offers.

"We don't need the money, Babe," George told her "I'm making enough to keep you playing amateur."

"I know," she responded soberly. "But I'd like to do a little bit on my own to help provide our security for the future. It isn't fair to let you do it all."

Finally an offer came from Hollywood asking her to make a series of ten short movies on golf and promising the huge sum of $300,000. She and George figured that the offers she had received, taken all together, would total half a million. Babe thought it over seriously.

"If I turn pro again," she said, "we'd have plenty of money to retire on. We could take a trip around the world. We could build that house I've always wanted. I think I have to do it."

And so in August she called a press conference and announced that she meant to turn professional again. At once more and more offers poured in. A sporting goods company wanted to market golf equipment to which she would give public approval, her name to appear on every product. One commitment that she made interested her immensely, that of designing dresses, shirts, slacks, culottes and shorts for women golfers.

"I'm going to love doing this," she told the president of the company as she signed her contract. "Women need sensible clothing that will allow them freedom of movement and yet let them look attractive. For years I haven't been able to buy such clothing, so I've designed and made all my own.

[*144*]

Now it's going to be fun to help other women."

With all her energy she threw herself into her new work as a professional. The movie contract did not materialize, although she later made three movie shorts for another studio. There were many exhibition matches all over the United States, and all of them paid good money. In one, held in the Yankee stadium in New York, she pitched to Joe Di Maggio; in another she put on a golf driving show with Ted Williams, baseball star of the Boston Red Sox. In fact, she had so many commitments that she knew she was beginning to tire from the strain and from so much traveling here and there. She felt that she could not rest, however; she had to keep her word to appear on schedule.

Her golf was suffering during this time also, and when she entered the Texas Women's Open that fall, she broke her long winning streak on this eighteenth tournament, managing after a hard fight to come in only second. Losing was such a blow to her pride that she worked harder than ever on golf, resulting in her winning the National Women's Open.

When she again complained to George that there weren't enough tournaments to keep her in trim for competition, he suggested, "Why don't we try to start a professional circuit for women? Like the one they have for men pros."

Both of them went to work on this idea, and in January of 1949 they were instrumental in organizing the Ladies' Professional Golf Association. Soon the women professionals had a number of tournaments, and their ranks increased from eight to thirty members. Now there were more chances for Babe to compete.

She did not always win, however. Often she would be the runner-up, but sometimes she would manage to make only the quarter or semifinals. There were too many commitments interfering with her practicing. She had a new position too, that of pro for the Sky Crest Country Club in Chicago, where she and George moved to live for a time. Although she enjoyed giving lessons, she had to spend long working hours at her teaching. A big honor came her way that year, however, to compensate her for her labors. The Associated Press voted her the Greatest Female Athlete of the first half century of the 1900's.

The next year she hit another winning streak, taking the prize money for first place in most of the big open tournaments. But by 1952 competition in the professional field was growing stronger. Sometimes Babe thought that it would be good just to sit on the club verandas and watch the younger girls play, for she knew that she was growing more weary each day. Besides, there was that tormenting pain in her side that bothered her all the time. In May when she was playing in Seattle, the ache grew unbearable. Although George, who was with her, begged her to drop out after the first eighteen holes, she refused to quit, dragging herself around the course, fighting what was now agony with all her will power until the tournament was finished. To her chagrin she came out in the eleventh place.

"I guess I'll have to give in and go to a hospital," she admitted to George. "I can't keep on losing this way, and I can't seem to win, fighting against pain all the time."

They flew at once to Beaumont to consult with the Didrikson family physician there, Dr. W. E. Tatum.

"It's nothing we can't fix, Babe," he told her after examination. "But you'll have to have surgery. It's a hernia—an organ protruding from the muscular wall around it. A few more days and it would have been too late for you."

After the operation she recovered too slowly, she thought, probably because she had been run down physically from all her exertions. She and George had bought a golf course of their own by this time, the Tampa Golf and Country Club in Florida. On the edge of the links there was a small caddy house which they remodeled for their own use. It was home to Babe, and it would be convenient now because here she could play a little golf every day and gradually increase her practice time.

Impatiently she kept telephoning Dr. Tatum to ask him when she could enter tournaments again. There was the All American coming soon, and after that the Worlds Championships and the Texas Women's Open, she told him. But in spite of all her importunities, the doctor would not give her permission to play until after the All-American was over. The other two she entered at once.

The World Championships came first, and she wanted particularly to win this tournament because she had taken it every one of the four times it had been held. People had begun to call it laughingly the "Babe Zaharias Benefit." In this one she had to excel. But in spite of good rounds the first and second days, she did not have the necessary strength to last out the play. By the third day she began to weaken, and she ended third to Betty Jameson and Patty Berg.

"Do you plan to quit now that the younger players are catching up with you?" a reporter asked her.

"Why should I quit?" she countered. "I'm just beginning to learn this game. I could play a lifetime and never know everything about golf."

To George she said, "I'm not too discouraged. It's what I have to expect, I guess, after that operation. But I'll win the Texas tournament."

"It's a tough course," he warned her. "Remember that's where you broke your big streak of seventeen victories."

"I'll win," she said.

And win she did. But afterwards it seemed harder than ever to recover her old power and zest. Nine holes was all she could take without wearing out. Nevertheless, she was determined to begin the 1953 circuit, and she did. She won once, managed to come in second a few times, and then dropped to a sixth place. When she finished a South Carolina meet not even in the running, she was so crushed that she was almost ready to give up. George, who was so worried about her health that he had been following her from tournament to tournament, kept trying to make her consult a doctor.

"But I'm really all right, honey," she would insist each time. "I'm just a little tired. Wait until we get to Beaumont for the Babe Zaharias Open. I promise to see Dr. Tatum then —after the tournament is over. I'm going to win this time."

She had to take that Beaumont Open, she told herself. Hadn't it been established in her honor? And in her own home town where everybody knew her and would be expecting her to win?

But when the play began, she realized that she was going to have a battle—not with her opponents, but with her own will to keep going. She was tired with a heavy dead sort of weariness that pervaded all of her, an exhaustion that seemed to come from within her. Every swing of her club took almost more effort than she could summon. The first two days she managed to take the lead, ending one stroke ahead of Louise Suggs, but the third and last day was steady torture.

What's the matter with me? Babe asked herself. I can't control my strokes. My drives seem to go where I don't want them to. I can't concentrate. I'd like to stop. But I won't. I won't.

Just before she teed off on her seventeenth hole, she saw her friend and protegé, Betty Dodd, a girl whom she had discovered playing good golf in Texas and had encouraged to enter the professional field. Babe and George were so fond of Betty that they considered her one of the family. Betty would tell the truth.

"What do I need to win?" Babe asked.

"Only two pars now. Just these last two holes," Betty answered, trying to sound encouraging although her face revealed her concern.

On the seventeenth hole Babe tried hard, but she missed making par because, with her ball only twelve feet from the cup, she was so fatigued that she had to take three strokes to sink it.

I have to have par on this last hole to tie the score, or a birdie to win, she thought. How can I do it?

Any movement was somehow too much of an effort to make. This was such exhaustion as she never had known—a deep inner lassitude that seemed to make all her muscles lax and turn her bones to rubber. If she ever had needed grit and stamina, it was now on this eighteenth hole with victory certain if—the big if—if only she could make herself hit the ball a few more times and hit it right.

Determination renewed, she stepped up to the tee and drove with all her ebbing strength. The ball sped, but it landed behind a tree. In some way she had to rise to the challenge of that trouble shot and send her ball up onto the green with one swing. She did it. Now for that birdie she had to have, that one stroke under par that she needed. Sighing, she took her putter and rolled the ball into the cup. She had done it. She had made her birdie and won the tournament.

Betty Dodd and Patty Berg came rushing from the crowd, boosted Babe on their shoulders, and carried her to the club house while the home town gallery cheered and cheered.

She was spent now, all her force drained from her. She was glad she hadn't let the Beaumont folks down, and that was all that mattered to her now except bed and rest and George's big gentle trainer's hands to rub the kinks from her tired muscles.

Chapter *12*

# A Need for Courage

The following morning Babe had an appointment to see Dr. Tatum, and as soon as his examination of her was over, she and George planned to drive to Phoenix for the next tournament on the golf circuit. She began to pack their bags but grew tired almost at once even from so small an exertion.

She felt that there must be something radically wrong with her to so sap the extraordinary vitality that always had been hers, and she preferred to face what might be sure knowledge of disaster by herself. She meant to keep trouble from George as long as she could. Two or three times lately the terrifying thought of cancer had entered her mind, perhaps because some years before she had seen Babe Ruth and talked to him in Florida. She had thought he did not look well. He had seemed so old and tired that she had not been surprised to learn later that he was dying of cancer. Often since then she had wondered if the too active life of an athlete might some day have a deleterious effect on her own health. All the way to the doctor's office she tried to talk herself out of a deep gloom of fear.

[*151*]

Just the same, while the doctor checked to see that everything was all right after her operation of the year before, she almost held her breath.

"It's okay," he said. "No bad results from your surgery."

"Then what makes me get so tired?"

He asked a few questions and then began to probe her abdomen. Watching in apprehension, she saw his face turn suddenly white. He had known her all her life, and she knew that he was fond of her. Now he was afraid, and his fear alarmed her anew.

"I have a cancer, haven't I?" she asked with her usual directness.

He did not answer her question. "Now look here, Babe, don't you go getting ideas. I'd like you to go to Fort Worth. There's a good specialist there—a proctologist. We'll have him take some tests."

Only a little something wrong, Babe thought. Then there was no sense in taking time out right now from golf for silly tests. She would just manage to rest more between tournaments until the season was over.

"But I can't bother with more examinations now," she said. "I have all kinds of commitments—exhibitions, tournaments, everything. Let's put it off for a while."

"No, Babe. Today," he insisted gravely. "I'll make all the arrangements."

All the way to Fort Worth she talked to keep from thinking, chattering about the birds whose bright wings flashed across the road, calling George's attention to the flowers she saw on the lawns of country homes. She wasn't

[152]

going to let him know her suspicions. Time enough for that when. . . .

The next morning Babe was cheered a little when she learned that the new doctor was also named Tatum, although she found on inquiry that he was no relation to her own dear Dr. Tatum. The new doctor did what he called a biopsy—took a small piece of tissue to study under the microscope.

"I'll have a report for you on Wednesday," he told her.

That was on Monday, and she had to live through two days of suspense before she would know. Still blanking the thought of cancer from her mind, she pretended a cheer that wasn't hers, but she could see that she wasn't fooling George much. He was distraught, pacing the floor.

The night passed somehow, and the next long day. When they went to the doctor on Wednesday, Babe was glad that at least now her suspense would be ended. He held out a hand to each, seated them, and then told them the truth quickly and candidly.

"It's—cancer, Mrs. Zaharias."

Ever since she had seen her own doctor's face turn white with concern, Babe had been trying to get herself ready for that verdict. Now when it came, it was like a sudden sharp stab of a knife. After that a stricken disbelief for a few minutes, then appalling fear. Blindly she reached out a hand toward George, and hers met his coming toward her to give strength and comfort.

"It's of the rectum," the doctor was continuing. "Not the fastest growing kind of malignancy." He went on to

[153]

explain about the types of cancer and the hope of surgery, ending with, "You'll need an operation."

"Doctor, will I be able to play golf again?"

He hedged, as she had been afraid he would. "Perhaps. Although I fear tournament golf would be too much of a strain for you. Golf just for pleasure, perhaps."

Babe scarcely listened while he went on to explain carefully exactly what the operation would do for her and the care she must exert in her recovery.

Going down in the elevator, she could not talk. When she glanced at George, she saw that tears were brimming in his eyes. Her own felt hot and dry. Tears wouldn't come— not yet. But when she was in the car, she broke down and wept. She didn't want her strong body tampered with. She didn't want that operation. But of course the cancer had to come out. She'd have to face that fact. And what was the matter with her, crying like this. She wasn't the weepy kind. Never had been. She wasn't going to cry again.

The next morning they left at once for Beaumont, for she wanted her own Dr. Tatum to see her through her trouble. On his kindness and love she could lean. Hope and moral strength had left her in spite of all her resolutions, and she was sunk deep in black depression again. In the car she saw her golf clubs. Snatching them out, she handed them to George.

"Here," she said bitterly. "Give these away. I won't be playing with them again—not ever."

He took them gently from her, putting them back in the car. "No, honey, no. You'll need them soon," he said.

Babe wept quietly for a time as they drove. This time she couldn't manage chit-chat about the birds and the trees. Her world was gray and murky. And then she was quite suddenly ashamed of herself, because all this gloom was only making their trouble harder for George to bear. After all, he must be her first consideration now.

"I'm going to stop this crying right now," she told him, sitting up straight and tall. "I've something real to tackle now. And we have things to discuss, arrangements to make."

All the rest of the way she talked and talked, although she scarcely knew what she was saying. She talked about letting her brothers and sisters know, about the tournament dates that must be canceled, about the kind of hospital room she wanted. But when a quiet time would come, she'd begin to think about her two cocker spaniels that she loved, about the home she might never build now, about the golf matches she would never play, about her good friends and her family who loved her. But most of all she thought about what would happen to George if she should have to leave him.

She entered the hospital where she had undergone her first operation, a Catholic institution called Hôtel Dieu. The House of God, Babe thought. Well, she was going to need God now as she never had needed Him in all her life before.

George had called Betty Dodd at her home in San Antonio, and Babe was glad when her friend rushed to Beaumont to help and comfort. She would understand about golf and about being afraid of the surgery that might mean the end of competition. There was Lillie too, who was Mrs. O. B. Grimes now, and living in Beaumont. Lillie would understand too, maybe not about golf, but about the dread of leaving George.

Dr. Tatum and George had agreed on a specialist to perform the operation, Dr. Robert Moore from the John Seeley Hospital in Galveston, and by this time the news was out in the papers. The world knew now why Babe Zaharias had not been winning tournaments.

Letters began pouring in, at first by handfuls and then by the basketful, until finally a nurse had to use a huge clothes hamper to hold them all each day. While George or Betty or Lillie read the messages, Babe lay propped against pillows to listen in touched gratefulness. There was a wire from her "sweethearts in the press sty" signed by forty-one newsmen, another from the Philadelphia Phillies, and one from the Boston Red Sox. Grantland Rice telegraphed, and Bobby Jones, and many others of her friends in the world of sports. Walter Winchell wired to cheer her by saying that he knew she was going to recover and that he'd never forgotten all the time and effort she had given to help other stricken people through the Damon Runyon Cancer Fund.

Flowers came by the boxful until Babe had to ask the sisters to take them around and share them with less fortunate patients. Since she could not possibly answer twenty thousand letters, she asked the newspapers to publish her thanks.

"Say that I'm grateful to all for the messages of cheer and hope," she told the reporters. "Tell them they're wonderful people and that it's a big help to know that folks all over the world are thinking of me. And tell them—just tell everybody 'Hello' from me."

She was further cheered when all her sisters and brothers arrived to be with her: Louis, Ole, and Arthur from their Texas homes, and even Dora and Esther Nancy from Arizona and California. Babe tried not to think that they had come because her case was serious; it was better just to concentrate on the fact that they loved her and wanted to be with her now that she was in trouble.

One day the doctors brought her good news: the x-rays had revealed no other trace of malignancy anywhere in her body.

The night before the operation, she whispered over the prayers she had learned as a child and had kept right on saying all these years. She told God that she didn't want her good useful body all changed around inside, but that she knew it had to be done. She asked for strength to go through with the operation.

"Please, God, give me spiritual muscle now," she prayed. "That's what I need."

She went to sleep after that sure that she was in God's hands and that she would now find courage to take what might come. In the morning when they were wheeling her out of her room, Dr. Moore came in. "Well, Babe," he said, "you're going to have a tough round today."

"I'm going to win it, and my whole big tournament too," she said gravely.

On the fourth floor at the door of the operating room, reporters and photographers waited.

[157]

*"Tell the world to expect me back to play golf," Babe said.*

"No pictures," George said, sounding gruff. "And no story."

But Babe lifted herself on one elbow and looked at the crowd. There was Tiny Scurlock of Beaumont, whom she had known since her high school days. There was an important message she wanted the papers to print, and Tiny would see that it went in.

"Tiny," she said, "tell everybody that I want them to pray for me. Tell the world to expect me back to play golf. And Tiny—tell them not to send me any flowers. Tell them to give the money to the Cancer Fund instead."

# Chapter 13

# A Hard Battle Won

**B**efore Babe went under the anaesthetic, a memory came to give her strength. She recalled one time when she had driven her ball into the rough so that it was lodged deep in grass, and there were trees all around to block the green. She stalked over, lips set in a grim line. The ball, she could see, was going to have to go through a small hole in the branches of the trees, an opening that was no more than fourteen inches wide.

"Hey, Babe, you aren't going to sock your ball through that little hole in the trees, are you?" an astonished spectator asked her. He measured the distance with his hand and added, "That place is only this wide."

She laughed and made a smaller circle with thumb and forefinger.

"Sure I'm going to try," she had answered him. "My ball's only this wide."

Now as the anaesthetists began their work, she thought

that her chances to get well again were no wider than that hole in the trees had been, but she would send the ball of victory through even the slimmest opening.

When they wheeled her back from surgery, she was conscious enough to know that George was beside her.

"Did they get it all out?" she whispered.

"Yes, honey. Four hours you've been on that table, but they got it. You're going to be all right."

For days she was only partially conscious. Sometimes she thought she was a little girl back on Doucette Street, jumping from the top of a big pile of sawdust near the old sawmill, and she was smothering in that dust. Again she would be in the high school auditorium, and some boy would start talking to her, and she would shush him, because it seemed to her that she had to have quiet. One day when she was conscious after sleep, she saw George sitting beside her bed smiling at her.

"Did you have a good game, honey?" he asked.

She couldn't answer because of the tube that hurt her throat and made it feel all raw and hot, but she asked a question with her eyes.

"You've been playing golf all the time you slept," he told her. "You moved your hands and feet right and kept twisting your neck. Just stay loose, honey, and we'll soon have you playing real golf."

"Stay loose" was what he always said to her before a big match, and now she told herself that if she could just keep relaxed, maybe she'd win this second and toughest round.

They took the tubes out about the sixth day, and after that she felt better, although she was still under drugs for a time. At last they told her she could get up and try to walk.

"So soon? I can't even sit up yet."

"I know," the nurse answered. "I'll prop you up, and you'll gain strength just from trying."

Babe was eager for any test that would bring her back to living. With the nurse holding her in a sitting position on the edge of the bed and then lifting her feet, she tried to take a step—and fell back weakly on the bed. Every day after that she kept making the effort, and every day it was a little easier to take a step.

One time she lay there wondering how a disciplined body like hers, the body of an athlete, could so yield to weakness. In the corner of her room stood her golf clubs where George had put them. In utter disheartenment she asked herself how she could ever play golf again, stride a course with her old vigor, send her ball winging down a fairway. And then she remembered asking God before her operation for the "spiritual muscle" to pull through. If spirit could win over body, as she had proved many times, then spirit now could bring back those flexible and responsive muscles of hers, restore power to her wasted body. Pushing back the covers, she examined her thin arms and legs.

"Sticks," she whispered to herself in disgust. "Just useless sticks."

But there was still muscle there. She could see it. Slowly she raised an arm and flexed it. Then—with difficulty—a leg.

[161]

If she could work at exercising those flabby muscles, tone and elasticity would return to them faster. Day by day she kept at it, gradually increasing the time of her efforts. There came a wonderful morning when she found that she could get out of bed without help. She could even walk as far as the corner of the room where her golf clubs had kept calling to her. Taking out an iron, she closed her fingers around the grip. Just holding that club in her hand felt right, felt marvelous too.

Back in bed after her exertion, she thought about all the golf courses she had played. The morning freshness of the air, the singing birds in the trees, the warm suns of afternoon, the smoothness of well-kept grass, the clean blue mountains of a West Coast background, the tang of the sea and the smother of fog at Gullane—these had been hers. The crack and whizz of a good drive, the satisfaction that came after a trouble shot well-played, the acclaim of a gallery, the fierce joy of winning against odds—worth working for indeed. And if determination and courage could bring them all back, she would have them again. And yet her body and sometimes her mind ached with the desire to give up, to let strength come again without all this grueling effort on her part.

Although recovery seemed endlessly slow to her, she knew and the doctors told her that she was gaining with each day. Now she could walk around her room and even out into the corridors. Often she glanced into the rooms of other patients to see men, women, and children far more ill than she was. Before long she stopped thinking about herself and began to consider what she might do to help others in the hospital and how she could bring hope to all ill people. If they could see visible proof that she was recovering, might it not bring cheer and encouragement to them? Her cancer operation had been much publicized. Why wouldn't stories in the papers about her recovery be effective?

She called a news conference, sending especially for

*She visited the sick children and told them stories.*

photographers and newsreel men. When they came, she was propped up in bed, setting her hair in waves.

"I washed it myself," she told the reporters proudly. "You can see I'm getting well. Please take pictures so that sick people everywhere can see that I'm recovering. I want them to know."

When she was a little stronger, she began visiting the hospital wards, where she talked with patients and sometimes played her harmonica for them, with Betty Dodd accompanying her on the guitar. Calls to the children's ward both hurt and inspired Babe, for she had not known that little ones could be victims of a disease such as she had. Why should they have to suffer in their tender innocence? She was always encouraged, however, when she saw their acceptance of pain, their faith in recovery. If they could disregard catastrophe, certainly she could continue her own fight toward health and vigor.

As she grew stronger, there were pleasant days when she could sit in the sun on the high hospital grounds to watch the distant boats on the gulf. There were drives also with George or Betty or Lillie.

Forty-three days after her operation, Babe was discharged from the hospital. When she said good-by to all the sisters, many of them cried, and she found that her own eyes were wet.

"I'll be coming back often," she told them. "I'm going to come to visit people who are sick like I was. I'm going to show them that they can live normal lives again."

Her brother Louis and his wife had a car waiting to take her to their home in Newton, where they were sure she would get her health back faster with all the good food they planned to feed her. George and the faithful Betty went with her, ready to help her begin the long battle toward living.

In Newton reporters and photographers were waiting.

"Let them come," Babe insisted. "I want to talk to them. I want them to put my story in their papers."

For a few weeks she rested in the sun, knitting, talking to friends, even painting a little, an art she had always wanted to try. Always she kept at her exercising, and gradually she gained weight and began to feel the joy of returning vitality.

"Let's go back to Tampa, George," she proposed in June. "I have to start practicing golf."

She called Dr. Tatum to ask him if she could begin working on her game, and was relieved and delighted when he said she could.

"Just take it easy at first," he warned.

The little pink stucco house on the golf course looked wonderful to her when she saw it. From room to room she walked, inspecting her huge collection of tarnished trophies that crowded the house even to the bathroom.

"Maybe I'll have time to get them under glass now," she told George. "I won't be winning any more cups for a month or so."

She admired the cheerful yellow of her kitchen and dining room and remarked how good it was to be in a house without inside doors.

"Doors just shut people away from each other," she said. "Happiness ought to have a chance to run in and out of every room."

From a window she looked out on the practice green and announced that she'd soon be working there. As the doctors had ordered, she began slowly, practicing her putts first because they needed skill, not power. Then gradually she added a few shots with her irons. There came a day when she played her first hole, still using a lighter iron instead of the heavy driver. The exertion tired her, however, and she had to ride back from the first green in a little electric car that George had bought her for use on the golf course. The next day she was jubilant when she managed to play a hole and a half and to walk home afterwards. The following day it was two holes.

George watched her vigilantly, scolding her for any overdoing that taxed her strength. When he had to leave for a business trip to Denver, he made her promise to be careful while he was gone. But one morning she woke feeling vigorous and airy, the way she always had when she was going to win a tournament. She had that wonderful sense of well-being, and she wanted to walk tall. Today, she resolved, she was going to play for a longer time.

Out she stalked to the golf course, teed off her ball, and played a startling nine holes without growing weary. Reporters watched her shoot a thirty-seven and ran for their news wires.

That night George called her from Denver, as she had known he would, for the papers had come out with big headlines, "BABE ZAHARIAS PLAYS NINE HOLES."

"What's this I read about you?" he asked, almost stammering in his concern. "What are you up to?"

Babe chuckled. "Honey, the paper's right. I played nine holes. And, man, I still feel wonderful."

"But, Babe," he scolded, and she could tell from his

voice that he was sick with worry, "it's been only three months since your operation. Can't you just go easy till I get home?"

"No, I can't. I'm going to enter the All American Open in July, and I have to practice. I'll need a lot of building up for that. But isn't it grand, George? All of a sudden I feel as good as new. We're going to be happy again. We're going to be able to live the way we always have."

In July of 1953, only three and a half months after her operation, Babe was at the Tam o' Shanter golf course in Chicago to compete in the All American. Hundreds of reporters, newsreel camera men, and sports columnists were there to watch her tee off, and she knew there wasn't a one of them who did not hope that she would be able to finish. George was there to follow her anxiously about the course, and she was paired with Betty Dodd by request. Betty would be ready to help if there was any difficulty. With only three full practice rounds behind her, Babe had persuaded herself that she must be ready for disappointment. This tournament was to be a test: if she could finish the course, play good golf, last for thirty-six holes, then she would have proved to all victims of serious illness that a comeback was possible for them as it had been for her. Of course she wanted to win. All those people in her gallery were hoping that she could, but she knew that they were also asking each other if The Babe could still play tournament golf and win.

With all her old fire and zest she stepped up to her tee for the opening drive, swung with all her strength, and sent her ball flying straight down the fairway for two hundred and

[*167*]

fifty yards. Sportswriters who had been saying that her career was finished clasped their hands over their heads as a sign of victory, people slapped each other on the back, and the whole gallery shouted and cheered.

Babe looked after her ball in pleased surprise. "Man," she muttered, "if I'd hit it any farther, it would have killed me."

After that first drive, however, nothing seemed to go right. Sometimes she could get distance on her drives, but not always; her chip shots never quite seemed to make the greens; her putting was unsure. She knew that she had lost control of her game. So taut with anxiety was her body that she kept getting into traps that made playing even more difficult. At the end of the first nine holes she had a forty-five, and her score for eighteen holes was a miserable eighty-two.

"It was ghastly," she told George that night. "But I know what was wrong. I was keyed up all tight."

But the next day was worse, and she ended her eighteen holes with a score of eighty-five. Heartsick but refusing defeat, she started the third day bravely. But everything was going wrong again, and what was worse, she was losing her confidence.

On the sixth tee she almost gave up. She cried a little on George's shoulder while he held an umbrella over her to hide her from the crowds. All of her was one big despair, one ache for surrender, and yet from somewhere came the moral courage to fight on.

"I'm going to pull myself together and play," she said, dashing away the tears angrily. "I won't have it be true—what they're saying about me—that I'll never play tournament golf again."

Both Betty and George urged her to pick up her ball and quit the match.

"I don't pick up my ball—ever," Babe said, and doggedly she began to play out the round.

Miraculously then her game began to come back to her, and she managed to finish the rest of the holes in two under men's par, ending the round with a score of seventy-eight.

The fourth day, however, all her strength seemed gone. No matter how she tried, she could make no better than an eighty-four. Heavy-hearted, she knew that she was far down in the running.

"Fifteenth place," she echoed when places were announced. "And tied for fifteenth at that. For me, that's just like finishing last, George."

"You're not strong enough yet. You've been pushing yourself too fast. Why don't you wait a while now? Not enter any more tournaments until you feel better."

"But I can't. Don't you see? I have to show people that I can come back."

Two days later Babe entered the World Championships on the same course. Although every swing of her club was strain for her, she finished the four days of play. At the end of the first three and a half matches she was actually ahead; then weakness and exhaustion proved too much for her and she began slipping behind. Her earlier play, however, had been good enough to land her in the third place behind Patty Berg and Louise Suggs.

Encouraged, Babe entered the Texas Woman's Open, only to be put out in the quarterfinals.

Her bitter disappointment was lessened somewhat by the many letters she received congratulating her on the brave battle she was putting up. She loved the messages from the people of the sports world, but even more she valued the letters from men and women ill with cancer who could now put hopeful words on paper because she had given them the desire to fight. Everyone of those letters she would answer, she determined. And how could she stop now, when what she was doing meant so much to others?

At the end of the year that had seen her operation and recovery, she was awarded the Ben Hogan Trophy for the Greatest Comeback of the Year of 1953. And she knew that it was an honor she had truly earned. Ben Hogan, who had offered this trophy after he had made an astounding comeback in golf from injuries received in a serious accident, would be glad that she had won his cup.

# Chapter *14*

# Back on the Circuit

The next year Babe was back on the golf circuit again, more determined than ever to win. Playing at Miami Beach in February, she fought Patty Berg for top place all through the first three days, entering the fourth and last match with a tie that continued through the first nine holes. Babe was all too aware that she was tiring, but she was so close to victory that she resolved to battle it out. Strength she might lack, she told herself, but unflinching persistence could keep whipping her on. Nine more holes to play, and if she lost one, she must win the next one. And so the see-sawing went on up to the very last hole, but try as she would Babe could not break that tie.

Just one more hole, she thought wearily. A long hole too, with a par of five, and to win it and take the tournament she could use only five strokes to reach the cup.

Teeing up her ball, she drove, aghast to see it land in a grove of palm trees. In the old days she would have wisecracked to her gallery, but not now. Now was a time for concentration, a time for dogged tenacity. Walking over, she inspected her trouble spot carefully. Palm leaves drooped to the ground all about the lie. Just beyond the grove was a sand trap.

Nothing to do, she thought grimly, but knock that ball right through those leaves and over the sand trap.

Taking a long four-iron, she swung with all the force and skill she could summon. And that sweet ball of hers tore through the leaves, soared well over the trap, and landed not too far from the green. Rejoicing, she strode to find her ball. And then she stood looking down, crushed, balked by that small round of white that now seemed to be conniving against her. There it lay, smug, triumphant—right in the middle of more sand.

I'll fix you, Babe muttered. I'll send you out of there good and hard.

Spurred on by irritation, she took a nine-iron and whammed that stubborn ball right up onto the green. Two skillful putts, and the ball was in the cup. She had played her eighteenth hole in par, and Patty hadn't managed to do so. The tie was broken, and the match was Babe's.

She was exultant because she had finally won a tournament. Now let the sportswriters change their yarns. Let them stop saying that she had lost her game. Babe Zaharias was back with a win now, and there would be more victories.

Although she kept on entering tournaments all that summer, she never forgot her resolution to do all that she could in the fight against cancer. In every town she played, she visited hospitals to seek out victims of the disease and to talk to them with words of cheer and hope. In a matter-of-fact tone she told them of her own operation and stressed her recovery.

"Look at me," she would say. "I'm the picture of health. I'm playing golf again, and winning too. If I can come back, you can do it too."

She also made long trips to give speeches for the cancer drives and played in many exhibitions to raise money to fight the disorder that attacked so many. Often she was too tired from her activities.

"You'll have to slow up a little, honey," George complained. "You're pushing nature too hard."

"But I'm as sound as can be. 'She looks and is the picture of vibrant health.' That's what somebody wrote about me."

"Sure. Sure. But you still get tired. You ought to give up something—either golf or all these trips for cancer work."

"Neither one of them. I can't give up golf. You know that. And—well, when I was so sick, I promised God that if He'd let me live I'd give of myself to all those others who need me."

Not long after her first victory, she was invited to go to Washington, D. C., to open the annual Cancer Crusade. In the White House, President Dwight D. Eisenhower was to press a button that would light up a huge sign in Times Square, New York. Babe was thrilled and happy because she knew that she would be presented to the President and Mrs. Eisenhower.

"Scared?" George asked.

"Me? Why?" Babe countered. "Ike's a golfer, isn't he? I'll know what to talk about."

Dressed in a light tailored suit and wearing one of her frivolous little hats, she presented herself at the White House with the committee that was to open the crusade. When the President was announced, she stood at attention with the others, a little sobered and impressed with all the ceremony. After that there was less formality, and she began to feel at home. When she met Mrs. Eisenhower, Babe pointed humorously to her own bangs and remarked, "Mrs. Eisenhower, I fixed up my bangs to look just like yours."

The first lady smiled graciously and, like any woman, responded with, "Oh, but yours look so pretty curled like that, Mrs. Zaharias. Mine will never curl."

The President flashed his famous smile as she shook hands cordially with Babe.

"How do you do, Mr. President," she said.

"How do you do, Mrs. Zaharias," he responded formally. And then, stooping he whispered with a grin in her ear, "Wait a minute after all this to-do is over, Babe. I want to visit with you about golf."

After the button was pushed and the photographers had taken pictures for the newspapers, Babe and the President of the United States talked golf.

"Some day we'll have a game together," he told her.

"Let's do," she responded and then added, laughing, "The way I'm playing nowadays, you just might beat me."

Babe was encouraged now that she was doing better with

her golf, although she was not winning any tournaments. However, she could always manage to be runner-up or to come in third. At least, she consoled herself, she wasn't down there in seventh or fifteenth place, and she was still up in the prize money class.

There was one tournament that she wanted especially to win—the 1954 National Woman's open. Twice now she had missed entering on account of her operations. This year she would compete, and she would win. Every day she practiced, knowing that the course at the Salem Country Club in Massachusetts was a difficult one and long. Before the opening date she and George went to Salem so that she could work out on the links in preparation.

On the first round she made a seventy-two, men's par for the course. On the second day she bettered her score and came out with a seventy-one, but in the morning round of the last day she dropped to a seventy-five. She was ahead, but she was concerned. Would she have the necessary stamina to play that second round of eighteen holes in the afternoon? Her back was hurting, and she knew that she had already spent her forces.

Summoning all her reserves of strength, she played out the afternoon, dropping only to a seventy-five. Jubilant, she knew that she had won the National Open—the most coveted title in all the professional golf circuit for women.

But in spite of her big victory, Babe soon began to realize that she was no longer the consistent winner that she had been before her operation. When tournaments came close together, allowing her no rest between, she did not have the endurance to play long rounds. Her work for the cancer drives was exhausting her more than ever now, for often there were long trips to reach commitments that she was determined not to refuse. One such was a journey across the continent to Seattle to open there a Babe Zaharias chapter of the American Cancer Society. Also there were television and radio appearances for the society and for the Damon Runyon Foundation.

"You'll have to cut down somewhere, Babe," George protested.

She sighed wearily. "I know it—now. I'm coming in fifth—even seventh. Let's quit the circuit for a while and go home to Tampa. I want to make beds and clean rugs and get my hands in dishwater. And I guess I do need a rest."

One morning soon after their arrival in Tampa, George woke her by shaking her hard. There was a big pleased grin on his face, and she thought perhaps he'd had another of his impulsive ideas about travel.

"Honey," he said "I've been going over figures. We're going to sell our golf club. And we're going to build that house you've always wanted."

"Could we? Could we honestly?" she asked, happier than she had been over winning the Nationals.

All her life she had wanted to own a home that she had planned herself, a home that would carry out all the ideas she had stored in her mind or tucked away on slips of paper. While she had been traveling around all over the country, she had studied the rooms in her friends' houses, deciding that she liked this room or that she wouldn't want that one.

Sometimes on long trips she had amused herself by sketching on paper the home that had always been her dream.

On the day they bought the land, she went with George to set out the boundaries for their home. It was to stand next to the golf course on a site overlooking a small lake. That day, just as they drove the last stake, a rainbow spread its fire of glory above the lake.

"It's an omen, honey," she said. "An omen of happiness. Let's call our home Rainbow Manor."

Everywhere she went after that, a pad, pencil, and ruler went with her, for she needed to use all her traveling time to plan her home. The kitchen, she decided, must be a push-button wonder, easy to work in. She didn't want any maid around. Away from home as much as she was, when she was there, she liked to do her own work, liked cooking for George. There would be a patio where they could have barbecue meals outdoors in the warm, sunny Florida weather. All the rooms must be large and roomy, because George needed space to make him happy and comfortable. Although this house was more her dream than his, he would live in it also and it must be planned for his ease. Everything would be on one floor too; no climbing up and down stairs. Happily she drew designs for every room, even marking in the windows before she turned her drawings over to an architect.

"It's a sort of a hybrid, Mrs. Zaharias," he told her, smiling over her plans. "A little mixed in origins—part California ranch house, part Colonial, with a little Pennsylvania Dutch thrown in. But we'll draw the blue prints for you."

"It's the way I want it," Babe said simply.

[177]

Although there was the planning and starting of the house to interfere with practice, in January she began playing the circuit, winning the first tournament, the Tampa Women's Open. It was not an easy victory. The usual weariness overwhelmed her on the last five holes, and she barely managed to keep one stroke ahead of Louise Suggs.

After that first win of the year, Babe began losing. One day in February she attempted to play a tournament in spite of the fact that she was sick with a virus cold. The first day's round was torture, her score a seventy-nine on an easy course. Although she started the second match she soon knew that she was too ill to play.

To a worried George she said, "I just can't seem to make myself play. The gallery expects me to win, but if I keep on, I'm going to disappoint them with a horrible score. I'm letting them down. Myself, too. I think I'd better quit."

And so for the first time in her golfing career she underwent what was to her ignominy—she picked up her ball and dropped out of the play, leaving George to handle the curious and concerned reporters who all wanted to know if she was seriously ill.

"Just a virus," he told them.

But it was more than that. When Babe went to Beaumont for her second cancer checkup, Dr. Tatum told her she would have to rest. Although there was no evidence of a recurrence, she was run down because she had been overworking.

"Why don't you just quit golf?" he asked.

"I'll rest, but I can't quit," she answered and then went on gravely to give her reasons. "You see, every time I do pretty well in a tournament, all the people who have had an operation like mine are encouraged to fight to recovery. I get hundreds of letters telling me that my comeback has given them hope."

She did rest, however, although the few weeks she remained away from the circuit were full and busy ones for her. With the new house nearing completion, there were electricians, decorators, and landscape architects to oversee. She was here and there and everywhere about the place, sometimes even helping to lay some of the bricks in the patio.

"Let's move in," she suggested to George. "Now's a good time—while I have to stay at home and rest."

"Rest? I haven't seen you do much resting. And we can't move in. The place isn't finished."

"That's all right. We can live in it. I just can't wait."

And so they moved in. George followed her around the house, and she knew that he was happy in seeing her joy as they walked from room to room to exult over every one of the features she had planned.

"Anything you want changed?" George asked.

"Not one thing. It's perfect just the way it is."

The house was still in an unfinished state when one day Babe's business manager, Fred Corcoran, called on her with a suggestion.

"Babe," he began, "for years people have been asking why you didn't write your memoirs. You've had an extremely interesting life, you know."

"Oh, Fred. You know I've never had time to do anything like writing."

[179]

"Well why not now—while you're resting?"

"But I'm busy with my new house. I can't take time to sit down and write a lot of stuff."

"You won't have to, Babe. We'll get, a tape recorder, and you can just talk into it. Sort of reminisce out loud."

She agreed finally, and the publishers who had already printed a handbook of hers on golf sent a writer, Harry Paxton, to help her tell her story. The tape recorder was set up and Babe began to talk, recreating aloud all the incidents of her life from childhood through basketball career and Olympics to her incredibly many golf triumphs. It was quite easy, she found, as she talked for hour after hour through her days, interrupting the story sometimes to settle some question for the builders who were putting the finishing touches on the house. The tape recorder came to seem like a friend to her, someone to whom she was telling all the wonderful things that had happened to her. In a way, it was like living over her whole life again, and she felt as if she were actually going through her experiences again. One day, when she was relating her story of her participation in that one-girl track team, telling about the "goosebumps" that had come all over her body as she ran out onto the field alone to hear the crowd cheering for her, she looked down at her legs below the shorts she always wore in the house. And there on her legs actual gooseflesh stood out.

"I guess I was really back there, Harry," she said, laughing. "I've been living it all again."

On and on she talked. Sometimes if she grew a little tired and the memories were hard to pull from her mind, a

"It's been a grand life," Babe said.

question from her helper would start the flow again.

"Do you suppose the book will be any good?" she asked Harry Paxton when it neared completion.

"I know it will, Babe. The public likes any book that's honest and revealing, warm with personality. You've been just yourself in telling your story—cheerful, natural, open-hearted. Anyone that reads this book is going to know the real Babe."

She was so pleased over what he had said that she told George about it that evening as they sat on their patio to enjoy the breeze blowing across the land from their lake.

He looked at her fondly. "Nobody in all the world can know the real Babe the way I do. Not from just reading a book. You're—the best."

She played with the long, silky ears of one of her cocker spaniels for a moment as she gazed out across the water.

"I'm so grateful for every single wonderful thing in my life," she said softly. "For my family, for golf, for my home—and for you. 'This Life I've Lived'—that's what my book is going to be called, George. And it's been a grand life. Do you know who I'm going to dedicate my book to?"

He grinned. "To golf I suppose."

"No. To you, honey—you. And to my father and mother, of course. But right on the flyleaf it's going to say: "To George, without whom there wouldn't have been any life."

Chapter *15*

# "A Wonderful Life"

**B**abe chafed all during the period of her enforced rest because she was not able to get in as much practice as she needed. Her many other projects kept her from the golf course. There was the new house, her autobiography, and the cancer work that she refused to abandon. Lack of practice she could correct, but another concern worried her. she no longer seemed able to concentrate on her golf game while she was playing. In order to win she had to be able to plan her shots, see the exact spot where she wanted to put her ball, and nowadays too many big problems in her mind seemed to get in the way of that concentration. Always there was the fear of the recurrence of the malignancy. There was the sagging weariness of her body that her mind had to work to conquer in every long match, that annoying matter of waning strength that would not allow her to finish a final round with her customary power.

For some time she had been realizing that the years must

bring the day when she would have to make over her golf technique, and now she decided that, although she was only forty-one, she must make that change. One of the secrets of her success lay in her careful effort to keep her ball away from trouble spots. That skill was all to the good, she knew. But through her early years of practice she had developed an aggressive manner of playing, always hitting down vigorously on her ball, whacking it energetically where she wanted it to go. Now she would build a new method, work for a smoother game that would require less effort and yet get results.

Painstakingly, patiently, she began to experiment, determined that she would not give up competitive golf, even if she had to play with less dramatic force.

That spring, her hopes high, she entered a tournament in Georgia, only to be chagrined and disheartened because she could make no better than sixth place. The same old weariness had kept her from doing her best. Although she was not due for her next cancer checkup for another month, she decided to go to the doctor for an examination.

"You need a real rest—away from home, out of sight of a golf course," the doctor told her. "All that's the matter with you is that you're run down and a little anemic."

This time she'd really rest, Babe resolved. She took a cabin with Betty Dodd on the coast of Texas. There they slept, ate big meals, loafed, fished, or just sat in the sun relaxing. One day when their car was stuck in the sand, Babe lifted and tugged to free it. Although her back hurt her a little at the time, she thought nothing of it. Rested and refreshed,

[184]

she went for her cancer checkup. There was no recurrence, and in her joy over that relief, she disregarded the aching back and returned to the golf circuit.

Her first tournament was the Babe Zaharias Open in her home town, the one she had always tried so hard to win because her victories pleased the Beaumont people. She had to take this one, she told herself, as she began play. But her back was hurting worse now, and fatigue was with her again. Her score on the last day was a heart-breaking eighty, and she ended in the thirteenth place.

"Will you quit now?" George asked, worried.

"Quit? No, I can't quit. Now I have to win at least one more tournament just to prove to myself that I can. I can't quit with a defeat."

She took vitamin injections and spurred herself on with the thought of victory. After losing one other meet, she did manage to take a contest at Spartansburg, South Carolina, winning by two strokes. Playing that day was torment for her, however. All through the four long rounds, she disregarded the excruciating pain in her back and kept fighting off the fog of exhaustion.

"Your eighty-fifth victory all told," George said as she staggered from the last green into his arms.

She smiled crookedly and did not answer. Only Babe Zaharias, she thought, was ever going to know what that victory had cost her. The pain in her back was an unendurable agony now. And she was tired, haunted and harried by leaden weariness.

Home to Tampa and bed she went. A little rest and

she would be alright once more, ready to go back and finish out the tour of tournaments with the other girls.

But instead of improving with rest, she soon knew that she was getting worse. In May she went to Galveston to consult Dr. Robert Moore, who had performed her cancer surgery. And to her overwhelming relief the agony in her back proved to be only a slipped disc, the result of her straining to tug her automobile out of the sand.

"Therapy, special exercises, and perhaps traction, and we'll have you back on your feet again," Dr. Moore told her.

After two weeks in the hospital and the discomfort of traction, with her legs pulled by weights to straighten her back, the pain was still with her. Again she had to undergo surgery, this time to heal a ruptured disc that the x-rays had revealed in her spinal column.

From her bed she smiled ruefully at George. "I'm not getting to enjoy our new home much, am I?" She laughed then. "Just you put my golf clubs up in the corner of this room again to remind me that I'll soon be back at golf."

She was filled with hope that enabled her to take the long hospital confinement philosophically, for now that the back was fixed, surely she would no longer be too tired to play that final round well. But one day Dr. Moore came into her room, his face sober.

"Babe, I hate to tell you this," he began, hesitated, and then went on brusquely. "We've found traces of recurring cancer."

At first she could not believe. Her bewildered glance went to George, who sat beside her bed, his head bowed, looking as if the world had stopped for him. Then she glanced at her golf clubs there in the corner of the room. Her eyes asked the doctor the question she could not find words to voice.

He nodded. "Yes, it's possible that you'll play again. There will have to be x-ray treatments of course. But in from three to six months we hope you'll be back on the golf circuit."

She summoned all her fighting spirit then. "Don't say it's possible. Say I will play again. Maybe I'll have a struggle getting out of the rough. But I'll beat this game yet."

Her resolve not to stop battling for health remained firm all those first few months, even when the pain grew so unbearable that the doctor had to operate to sever the nerves that transmitted feeling from her legs. For five and a half hours she was in surgery, but when she came out from under the anaesthetic, she was still clinging tenaciously to hope.

"They stopped the pain," she said. "Now I'll be able to get better."

Knowing that George suffered when she did, for he had told her, "When you hurt, I hurt," she tried to conceal the agony that kept returning. When he was with her, she talked for hours about all the fun they still were going to have together.

"I won't enter very many tournaments," she told him. "Maybe just one or two of the big ones each year. We'll have more time together. I'll be at home more. And well take that trip around the world that we've always wanted to have."

When he read to her the messages she received from all

[187]

over the world, she would say, "I'm so grateful for all our wonderful friends. I'll make another comeback. How can I fail when all these good friends are expecting to see me playing golf again?"

As the winter holidays drew near however, Babe began to suspect that she was losing her battle, for she seemed to be no better. There was still the pain. Often she thought of that first Christmas Eve that she and George had spent together after their marriage. She had been so strong then, so happy that it had seemed as if clouded times could never come. To go back to that beginning might give her renewed will power not to give up.

The day before Christmas, she asked George, "Do you suppose I could spend tomorrow out of the hospital? Maybe we could go to the Bowens. Please call them and ask if they'll take us in again."

She saw George glance questioningly toward one of the doctors who happened to be in her room, saw the doctor shrug his shoulders. What did that shrug mean? That it didn't matter what she did now?

"Of course she can go," he said cheerily. "Christmas in a hospital isn't much fun for anyone."

The Bowens came at once when George telephoned them, flying their private plane from Fort Worth so that Babe could ride in comfort. George lifted her and carried her into the plane where a bed had been made for her. All of the short flight from Galveston she found it hard to keep smiling, but she kept all evidences of her suffering from the others. After all, she was learning now to live with pain.

[188]

All of Christmas Day she made herself laugh and chatter, trying not to look down at her wasted body, trying not to remember how strong and athletic, how responsive to every demand that body had been on the snowy evening nineteen years ago when she had followed George through the blizzard to find an empty home that had meant warmth and food and comfort.

When Bertha Bowen called them to Christmas dinner and George carried her to her chair, Babe laughed in delight, although there was a catch in her breath. For there in the center of the table stood a great bowl of pork and beans. Of course there was a huge turkey at one side of the bowl, sweet potatoes on the other, and all the Christmas "fixings" spread around.

"The best of all is the pork and beans," Babe insisted. "Better to me than the turkey. Do you remember, George?"

The months moved slowly on. In March Babe was told what she had feared was true. The malignancy had spread. The doctors had done all they could. She was matched now with a foe she could have no hope of defeating.

With steadfast courage she met the tragic knowledge that she could not win back to living. No effort on her part could make victory hers. But because her opponent was stronger than she was did not mean that she was going to "pick up her ball and quit." She would fight on as long as she could. More and more of that "spiritual muscle" for which she had often asked God would have to be hers now. And perhaps He would give her the courage to stop thinking of herself now, stop feeling sorry for herself because she

[189]

would never play golf again. Now she must think of George and of all the others who might need her.

"George," she asked one day, "couldn't we set up a fund for cancer research? We have more money than we need. I'd like to think that some day, perhaps a little through our help, science will find a way to cure cancer."

"Anything you want, honey," he promised. "And as much as you want."

"Then I'd like to establish a Babe Zaharias trophy to be awarded each year to the best woman athlete. Perhaps it would encourage the younger ones to keep climbing."

Babe talked about all the other patients in the hospital, inquiring for those who had recovered and gone home and for those who lay near death. She talked about the doctors and the nurses, who were doing all they could to ease her own pain.

"They work so hard," she said. "All the doctors and nurses. They're so good to me. I wonder if they ever get enough rest. I guess I'll have to try to eat more so that I won't worry them. I must do what I can to help."

Another day she told George, "I've had a wonderful life. Everything I've ever wanted has been mine. Success, wealth, a home, friends—and you."

"Because you fought for what you wanted, Babe. You always fought."

She smiled. "Never for you, George. Never for friends. The best things I've had just came. I guess winning friends—and love—is a lot better than winning golf championships."

Early in September, Babe was warmed and cheered by

a letter from one of those friends she'd made, a letter from President Eisenhower. He wrote:

"This is just a note to say the whole country unites . . . in admiring your courage. . . You have been an inspiration to all Americans."

On September 27, 1956, Babe Didrikson Zaharias lost her last round in her long battle with death. Peacefully and in her sleep she died.

"She'd had enough," George said.

And the President of the United States said, "Everyone feels sad that finally she had to lose."

But in a way, Babe did not lose, for the example of her courage and her determination lives on in the hearts of all young athletes.